This book is dedicated to the victims of the Beirut blast on August 4, 2020, and to all Lebanese, near or far, who continue to suffer the consequences of Lebanon's current crisis.

Also by Barbara Abdeni Massaad
*Man'oushé: Inside the Lebanese Street Corner Bakery*
*Mouneh: Preserving Foods for the Lebanese Pantry*
*Mezze: A Labor of Love*
*Soup for Syria: Recipes to Celebrate Our Shared Humanity*

# FOREVER
# BEIRUT

## Recipes and Stories from
## the Heart of Lebanon

Written and photographed
by Barbara Abdeni Massaad

*Foreword by Chef José Andrés*

Interlink Books

First published in 2022 by

Interlink Books
An imprint of Interlink Publishing Group, Inc.
46 Crosby Street
Northampton, Massachusetts 01060
www.interlinkbooks.com

Library of Congress Cataloging-in-Publication
Data available
ISBN 978-1-62371-853-4

Publisher: Michel S. Moushabeck
Editor: Leyla Moushabeck
Book design: Harrison Williams and Maria Massaad
Cover design: Harrison Williams
Photo editing: 53dots.com
Proofreaders: Jane Bugaeva and Jennifer Mckenna

Printed and bound in Korea
10 9 8 7 6 5 4 3 2 1

To download our complete 48-page, full-color catalog,
please visit our website: www.interlinkbooks.com,
or e-mail: info@interlinkbooks.com.

# CONTENTS

# FOREWORD

In some ways, Lebanon has been in my heart for a long time, ever since the days I started learning about the cuisine as we prepared to open my restaurant Zaytinya, in Washington, DC. But my love for the country was never as real as it became in August of 2020, when the entire world looked on in sadness and horror as the unthinkable happened: a massive explosion in the Port of Beirut. Our team started cooking quickly and coordinating with a group of local restaurants to make sure that the army of incredible volunteers working to clean up the city could eat. Women and men, many of them young, and all of them driven—people showed up to support each other, no matter what. I truly saw the spirit of Beirut.

But a message that I heard again and again was that the people of Beirut no longer want to always have to be resilient. It's a word that's used a lot to represent the strength and drive that can be seen in so many communities after disasters. In Beirut, to add a terrible blast on top of Covid-19, on top of deep economic troubles—it just isn't right. Young people deserve better. They should be growing up in a world that they can shape in their own way, not restricted by the constant need to be "resilient." They just want to live their lives. And yet, what I felt in Beirut in those first few days after the blast was the sense of a big family coming together as one to accomplish something bigger than themselves. And, of course, every conversation began and ended with food.

The shared language of Beirut is its cuisine and its hospitality. Even in the midst of such destruction, I was welcomed with open arms to markets, shops, restaurants, and homes—to taste a new flavor, to try a bite of bread with za'atar, or a tomato salad.

Barbara Abdeni Massaad, with help from my friend Kamal Mouzawak, paints this image of Lebanon as being like a bowl of tabbouleh, the diverse ingredients "distinguishable but never separable..." This is, to me, the beauty and strength of the country, and what will help it survive its current crisis, as it has survived others for generations. When young people come together and unite, things can get better. And they will get better. Hopefully someday in the very near future, these young people will no longer need to be resilient day in, day out. They will be able to fully live and thrive.

*Forever Beirut* beautifully captures the spirit of Beirut, of its communities, cultures and languages, of this "tabbouleh city" coming together to support itself. And it's not only about Beirut. It is a global book, connecting every city and country that has been touched by immigration of the Lebanese people. This is what we can hope for, a tabbouleh planet, uniting to support its most vulnerable, each community distinguishable but never separable. It's a big wish, but if we can all take inspiration from the heart of Lebanon, maybe we can get there.

—*Chef José Andrés*

# WHY *FOREVER BEIRUT*

On August 4, 2020, a massive explosion shook the port of Beirut—and with it, my world and the worlds of all who love Lebanon. The blast reached over half the city, damaging homes up to six miles away, leaving more than 200 dead, over 7,000 injured, dozens missing, and 300,000 homeless (source: Human Rights Watch). But its aftershocks also hastened an unraveling of the country's fabric that has been going on for years.

Political instability, unemployment and poverty, the Covid pandemic on top of a refugee crisis, shortages of basic necessities such as gas, electricity, housing, medical care, and food—the country seems to be hurtling toward the abyss.

But like other countries in the region and our world, Lebanon has faced disasters before. And as Fairuz's popular song reminds us, how can we help but love our homeland? So, like anyone who loves and cares about the city of Beirut and Lebanon, how could I not try to do something? And the way I lend a hand—and my heart—is with food.

I write cookbooks, so I decided to work on a book highlighting 100 recipes of our culinary heritage, to conserve and safeguard this treasure. I wanted the book to help share our culture and to raise funds to support the work of the Lebanese Food Bank, who are doing such great work feeding families in need during these dire times.

I chose recipes that are the most common and more or less easy to make in your home kitchen. The book includes sections on soups, salads, breads & savory pastries, mezze, kibbeh, grills, main dishes, preserves & pantry staples, and sweets.

I have also written text—personal stories—and taken photos for each recipe. I portray our culture with my affection and nostalgia for the old Beirut, mixed with our present fate, through words and images that are raw, fragile, sensitive, shocking, emotional, and true. The streets of Beirut never cease to inspire me, offering glimpses of faces of the many different communities of this country and reflecting the emotional roller-coaster ride we are living on a daily basis.

A recipe is so much more than just a set of ingredients or a to-do list. It can be a custom that brings us to our senses, enabling us to reflect on, embrace, and preserve the ties that bind us. All the tiniest steps described in preparing these dishes are small, indispensable gestures of caring in which cherished memories of trust and of closeness to loved ones are stored for safe keeping. My hope is that remembering and retracing them may help heal and renew us, in times like these.

—*Barbara Abdeni Massaad*

# INTRODUCTION

Does Beirut still exist?
Did Beirut ever exist?
Since its birth, Beirut is in perpetual reconstruction and reinvents itself permanently.
—Nadia Tueni

Lebanon has a bewildering geographical, climatic, biological, and human diversity, made of an entangling social string of different religious, political, and communal affiliations. This striking diversity has given birth to one of the most acclaimed and varied cuisines in the world. The cuisine expresses not only the taste of its people but also its culture, traditions, heritage, and aspirations—it welcomes influences from faraway lands while protectively preserving its soul and identity. It embodies the spirit of the land that shapes it, carrying its colors and flavors with a wide range of dishes. Food is the most prominent factor that links us all as Lebanese.

I have traveled throughout Lebanon for many years, reaching out to people of all communities, to learn about our food and practices. They have always been welcoming, without exception. Well almost...

I was visiting my friend, Abou Kassem, in Zawtar, a village in South Lebanon, to learn about every aspect of za'atar—from seed to the final mix, which we eat extensively in our daily meals. I took photos throughout the day. As I was heading home, I saw a charming sign on the road near Nabatieh. The sign displayed an illustration of garlic, and advertised a snack bar serving sandwiches. I stopped the car and took out my camera, which had the telephoto lens attached. Since the sign was so far away, it made sense to use it to capture the image.

Suddenly, a man from a local militia appears out of nowhere, screaming at me and threatening to destroy all the photos on my memory card. I raised my hand to halt his shouting, smiling of course. I pulled out the book *Man'oushé*, which luckily was tucked in the pocket of the back seat of my car, and started showing him the photos, slowly, one by one. His jaw dropped. He might have been hungry. I assured him that I have never been interested in politics, and especially not in espionage. Suddenly, a grin came over his face, banishing his mistrust, and he shouted with great pride.

"My mother is the best cook!"

Frankly, I was not expecting these words.

He strongly insisted I come with him to taste her food. I was embarrassed to let him down, although deep down I was very curious. But it was getting late, and I had to return home to my family. Before leaving, I joked with him, "*Ken lezem tahkineh hayk min el awal*, you should have spoken to me like this right from the start."

This episode clearly defines for me our relationship to food, and to one another, as Lebanese. Food is a powerful, benign force that can disarm all kinds of hostility. It could become a great instrument for leaders to use to bring peace to our part of the world.

I will keep dreaming...

Traditional life in Beirut is under constant threat. Its gastronomy is not. Lebanese cuisine continues to play the important role of an ambassador to our country. Lebanese food combines pleasure, balance, and health. You can eat quickly on the go or take your sweet time sharing a moment of conviviality, socializing around a table full of mezze with family and friends for hours. The pretext of meeting around a table for a meal undoubtedly reflects the warmth and art of living of the Lebanese, whose soul is linked to that of the people of the Mediterranean.

Rummaging through old books on Lebanon, I came across a passage that romantically expresses the splendor of our Lebanese cuisine.

> How to speak about Lebanon without evoking its phenomenal gastronomy… Rich as the sun illuminating its vines, olive trees, and citrus fields… *Elegant* in the image of its snow-capped mountains and its thousand-year-old cedars… Sensual like an oriental rose, seductive, generous, sweet, fragrant, and original.

The 100 recipes in this book represent a qualitative attempt to showcase our cuisine. It is by no means a representation of all the dishes we eat in Lebanon. I have included the recipes that most Lebanese put on their table all around the country, and to be honest, the ones I love the most.

*Sahteyn wa hana!* Twice to your health—with joy!

# SOUPS

# SOUPS

## *Shorba*

I have been searching for warm, comforting food ever since I was a child. I remember one time when I was ten years old I told my father, "Soup warms my heart." This feeling has lingered throughout my adult life.

When researching for my cookbooks, I have always found true comfort in visiting rural areas, cooking and eating with farmers and small-scale producers. Soups in the past were often the base of their daily food. I dedicated one of my cookbooks to the subject: *Soup for Syria*, a collection of soup recipes from all over the world, including those of famous chefs and food writers, to raise money for Syrian refugees.

One of the first films I ever watched, in grade school in the mid-seventies at Saint Joseph College Antoura in Lebanon, was Charles Dickens' *Oliver Twist*. The scene I remember most is when Oliver queues with his bowl to be served a thin soup to ease his hunger. And when he asks audaciously for more, I could relate to his needs, as I was a voracious eater too at the time. I can still picture the ladle dipping slowly into the steaming cauldron.

Soup is the perfect healthy food for today's hectic lives, considering of course that you use seasonal ingredients to cook it. My favorites are whole meal soups which are rustic in spirit, robust in flavor. When I became a mother, it was important to provide warm nourishment for my family—the large pot filled with soup which had simmered brought us together on the table in communion. French chef and culinary writer Auguste Escoffier writes beautifully about the characteristics of a good soup. "Soup puts the heart at ease, calms down the violence of hunger, eliminates the tension of the day, and awakens and refines the appetite."

A few years ago, I was invited as a guest chef at Berlinale, Berlin's International Film Festival and one of the largest public film festivals in the world. The invitation corresponded to the book launch of *Soup for Syria* in Germany. I was asked to do Lebanese lentil soup—*shorbet addas bi hamod*—for guests during the festival. I made a huge pot to feed hundreds of people. I was so proud to be serving this recipe from Lebanon in Germany. I got energized and wanted to live the full experience, so I declined any help when it came to serving the soup to guests. It was a very humbling experience I will never forget, especially the kind words of appreciation I heard once people tasted the soup. I have to admit that at the end of the night, my hands were very sore.

**Left:** "I love you when you bow in your mosque, kneel in your temple, pray in your church. For you and I are sons of one religion, and it is the spirit."—Kahlil Gibran

# Lentil and Swiss Chard Soup with Lemon

## *Shorbet Addas bi Hamod*

Lentils are an important staple in Lebanese homes. This hearty soup is full of goodness: lentils, chard, potatoes, and tangy lemon juice. I like to add carrots and a big bunch of fresh cilantro too. For maximum flavor, the garlic is fried in olive oil before adding it to the soup towards the end of cooking; a method called *taqleyeh*. You can make the soup thick like a stew, as we prefer it in Lebanon, or add more water for a thinner consistency. To give it extra texture, you can serve it with fried or toasted Arabic bread, broken into pieces.

Every time I cook this soup I think of my son, Albert, who is now a trained chef. Even as a child, food was everything to him. As soon as he stepped out of the school bus, he would run home and ask, "What will we eat today?" If I was making *shorbet addas bi hamod*, he would cry with frustration (though now he eats it with pleasure!). This soup remains one of my favorite dishes to cook for my family.

2 cups (400 g) brown lentils

Extra-virgin olive oil

1 medium onion, finely chopped

3 carrots, sliced (optional)

1 bunch Swiss chard, leaves and stems chopped separately (or use kale, radish greens, turnip greens, or spinach)

2–3 medium potatoes, peeled and cut into large cubes

1 tablespoon salt, or to taste

1 tablespoon flour, mixed with ¼ cup (60 ml) water (optional)

2–3 garlic cloves, minced

1 bunch cilantro, leaves finely chopped

Juice of 1 lemon, or to taste

Arabic bread (p. 28), toasted or fried and broken into pieces, to serve

Lemon wedges, to serve

Spread the lentils out on a tray and pick through them to remove stones or impurities. Rinse under cold running water and drain.

Heat 1 tablespoon of olive oil in a large pot and sauté the onion until soft, but not browned. Add the lentils to the pot, along with 6 cups (1.5 liters) water, or enough to cover. Bring to a boil over high heat then lower the heat and simmer until softened, but still firm in the middle, about 25 minutes.

Add carrots (if using) and Swiss chard stems, and simmer for 5 minutes. Add the potatoes and salt, and continue to simmer for an additional 10 minutes. For a thicker texture, stir the flour mixture into the soup until well blended, 5 minutes. Stir in the Swiss chard leaves and continue to cook for 10 minutes, or until the leaves wilt and the lentils and vegetables are soft.

Heat 2 tablespoons of olive oil in a small frying pan and fry the garlic until it starts to sizzle. Mix in the cilantro and stir into the soup.

Remove from the heat and stir in the lemon juice. Serve with a drizzle of olive oil, Arabic bread pieces, and lemon wedges on the side.

# Chicken Soup

## *Shorbet Djej*

I don't need to tell you the benefits of a good chicken soup—it nourishes both the body and soul for so many cultures around the world. Cinnamon is the fragrant twist that makes our version special. You can also add cloves, nutmeg, fresh ginger, or cardamom seeds for extra spice. We cook chicken soup for our families during cold winter nights, especially when someone needs comfort and a boost to the immune system. The warmth and flavor of the soup will lift your spirits, and, in the end, that's all that matters.

5 lb (2.25 kg) free-range whole
   chicken or chicken pieces

1 large onion, coarsely chopped

1 cinnamon stick

3–4 allspice berries

2–3 black peppercorns

1 tablespoon coriander seeds

1 bay leaf

1 tablespoon coarse sea salt

1 tablespoon butter

1 cup (100 g) broken vermicelli
   (made from durum wheat)

2 small zucchini, coarsely chopped

2 large leeks, white and light green
   parts only, coarsely chopped

3 carrots, sliced

1–2 celery stalks, with some leaves,
   finely chopped

1 tomato, coarsely chopped

1 small bunch flat-leaf parsley,
   coarsely chopped

1–2 lemons, zested or
   cut into wedges for squeezing

In a large stockpot, place the whole chicken and cover with 12 cups (3 liters) of water. Bring to a boil over medium-high heat, skimming the foam from the surface. Reduce the heat to a simmer and add the onion, cinnamon stick, allspice, black peppercorns, coriander seeds, bay leaf, and salt. Simmer, partially covered, for 45 minutes until the chicken is cooked and the broth is fragrant. Continue to skim off the foam, if needed.

Lift the chicken from the broth and set aside on a plate. Strain the broth through a fine sieve or cheesecloth and set aside to cool. Reserve the chopped onion. You can make the broth a day ahead (once chilled, the solidified fat can be removed from the surface, if you wish).

Returning to your chicken, remove and discard the bones, cartilage, and skin. Separate the chicken meat into bite-size pieces.

In a small frying pan, heat the butter and brown the vermicelli, stirring, until evenly golden. Remove from the pan immediately, as it can burn quickly. Set aside.

In a large soup pot, combine the broth, zucchini, leeks, carrots, celery, tomato, and parsley. Bring to a boil, then turn down the heat and simmer for 15 minutes, until the vegetables are tender. Add the chicken pieces, vermicelli, and lemon juice or zest and heat through. Taste and adjust the seasoning, if needed. Serve hot, with lemon wedges alongside if desired.

# Lamb Shank and Vegetable Soup

*Shorbet Mawzet wa Khodra*

This soup is proof that you can make a delicious meal with a small amount of meat and lots of fresh vegetables. Dishes like this came out of a time when meat was scarce and a luxury for families. Lamb was, and is still, the first choice. My husband, Serge, often tells me stories of his grandmother Marie, who would feed the whole family with vegetables from the garden and just a few pieces of meat. She would send someone to buy the meat while she washed and cut the vegetables. The soup would boil for a long time, but was always ready in time for supper and there was always enough to go around.

I am reminded of the old European folk tale Stone Soup, where hungry travelers persuade villagers to come together to make and share a meal. This lesson of collaboration and teamwork is especially powerful as, for many, it is a time of scarcity once again.

1 lb (450 g) boneless lamb shank, cut into chunks

1 tablespoon coarse sea salt

1–2 bay leaves

1 cinnamon stick

1 onion, peeled and spiked with 4 cloves

1–2 celery stalks, with some leaves, finely chopped

3 medium carrots, sliced

2 small zucchini, cut into large cubes

2 medium ripe tomatoes, peeled and coarsely chopped

¼ cup (50 g) short-grain white rice, soaked in cold water for 30 minutes

Pinch freshly ground black pepper

1 small bunch flat-leaf parsley, finely chopped

Place the lamb in a large pot, along with 10 cups (2.4 liters) water, or enough to cover. Bring to a boil over medium-high heat, skimming the foam from the surface. Reduce the heat to a simmer and add the salt, bay leaves, cinnamon stick, and onion. Cover and simmer for 45 to 50 minutes, until the lamb is tender, adding extra water during cooking, if needed. Remove the bay leaves, cinnamon stick, and onion. (You can make the broth a day ahead—once chilled, the solidified fat can be removed from the surface, if you wish. Just return it to a simmer and proceed with the recipe).

Add the celery, carrots, zucchini, and tomatoes to the broth and simmer until just tender, 10 to 15 minutes. Drain the rice, add it to the pot, and continue to simmer until the rice and vegetables are cooked, about 10 minutes more. Season with the black pepper, and more salt, if needed. Serve hot, garnished with chopped parsley.

# Kishk Soup

## *Kishkiyeh*

*Kishk* is a fine powder made by fermenting and drying a mixture of cracked parboiled wheat (bulgur) and yogurt made from cow or goat milk. It is skillfully fermented by small-scale producers until the mixture sours, then it is dried in the sun and rubbed periodically to a fine powder. Through this method, the yogurt is preserved without needing refrigeration. Outside of Lebanon, you can find it in well-stocked Middle Eastern grocery stores under the names *kashk*, *kishk*, *jameed*, or *tarhana*, depending on its origin.

Lebanese people have a love-or-hate relationship with *kishk*—it's a well-known fact. I am obsessed with *kishk*—there, I said it! When I was ten years old, my family and I immigrated to the United States to Fort Lauderdale, Florida, where my aunt and her family lived. Eight years later we returned to Lebanon, and *kishk* was the first unfamiliar food I tasted upon our return. My mother was so excited to cook this soup for us. I loved it! It has a rich, distinctive sour cheesy flavor.

Kishk soup is often cooked with *awarma*, a traditional spiced lamb confit, or simply seasoned with fried onions and garlic. I tasted a delicious version made by Zeina Hamady, a cook from the Chouf, the heartland of the Lebanese Druze community south-east of Beirut. She used spices and edible wild greens from her backyard to make her *kishkiyeh*, inspiring me to make my own.

1 teaspoon coriander seeds

2 tablespoons extra-virgin olive oil

1 medium onion, sliced

Pinch salt, if needed

1 teaspoon red pepper paste (p. 200)

1 tablespoon tomato paste

1–2 garlic cloves, minced

1 large potato, peeled and cut into small cubes

1 cup (100 g) *kishk*

1 small bunch Swiss chard, leaves chopped (or use kale, radish greens, turnip greens, or spinach)

4 tablespoons *Awarma* (Lebanese Lamb Confit, p 197) or cooked ground lamb (optional)

Arabic bread (p. 28), to serve

Toast the coriander seeds in a dry frying pan set over medium heat to bring out their full flavor. Using a mortar and pestle, crush the seeds, pressing and moving the pestle over them in a circular motion.

In a pot, heat the olive oil over medium heat and sauté the onions until translucent. You can add a sprinkle of salt to help soften the onions faster, but be careful not to add too much, since *kishk* is usually quite salty.

Stir in the crushed coriander, then the red pepper and tomato pastes. Stir for about 2 minutes, until well blended. Add the garlic and cook, stirring, for 1 minute. Add the potatoes and stir well to ensure they are fully coated in the mixture. Pour in 2 cups (480 ml) of water and bring to a boil, then turn down the heat and simmer for about 10 minutes, until the potatoes are cooked but still firm. Whisk in the *kishk* and, whisking constantly to prevent scorching and lumps, cook for 5 minutes until blended. Add the greens and continue to stir with a wooden spoon for 10 minutes. Add a little water, if necessary, until the soup is your desired consistency; it should be creamy and thick.

If you are lucky enough to have *awarma*, melt it in a small frying pan, stirring, then pour off the fat if desired. Garnish the soup with *awarma* or cooked ground lamb, if desired. Serve with Arabic bread—Lebanese people love to use bread as a utensil.

# SALADS

# SALADS

## *Salata*

Lebanon's Mediterranean climate is very favorable for growing vegetables and fruit. On average, we can expect 300 days of sun a year. The result is fresh produce bursting with color and flavor. Fresh seasonal vegetables are served at every meal, including breakfast, either salads or a selection of raw vegetables. The *"jat khodra,"* a basket full of fresh vegetables, is served at the beginning of a lavish mezze spread to open one's appetite. The varieties of salads are numerous. Tabbouleh and *fattoush* are the most popular.

Physician and environmentalist Dr. Antoine Daher even compares Lebanon to tabbouleh (as quoted by Kamal Mouzawak, founder of Lebanon's first farmers' market):

> Tabbouleh is a mix of diverse ingredients, where one can distinguish every single one but can never separate the one from another. It's just like this country, made of such diversity and differences, all very distinguishable but never separable.

As a child, I did not particularly like salads. I can still remember sitting at the table for hours trying to swallow "leaves." This situation changed radically as I became a teenager. When I worked in my father's restaurant, Kebabs and Things, in Florida, I would eat tabbouleh every single night. I became addicted. Salad became one of my most essential foods as I became an adult, especially once I returned to Lebanon. Every day I would eat a huge bowl of fresh romaine salad with a simple dressing made of lemon juice, extra-virgin olive oil, and salt. A very good friend of mine questioned this daily indulgence, finding it very unusual.

When my family immigrated to the United States, my fifth-grade teacher, Mrs. Eden, at Florida Oaks School, asked me to make a national dish from Lebanon to serve to our class. My mother made a huge bowl of tabbouleh, which I brought to my classmates. I wore a beige-colored *abaya* (a long traditional robe) for the occasion. I felt very proud that day. Throughout my life, I would continue to showcase the best of our cuisine.

**Left:** In the old neighborhoods of Beirut, traditional hand-woven baskets dangle down from high balconies of longstanding buildings awaiting goods from food peddlers.

# Tabbouleh

Tabbouleh is a quintessential part of Sunday lunch, a ritual in most Lebanese households, especially during summertime. Families gather around to taste the tabbouleh just before it is served to make sure that the balance of lemon, olive oil, and salt is perfect. It's a joyful dish.

The main ingredient in tabbouleh is parsley. No parsley, no tabbouleh! The salad should be predominantly green, with subtle specs of red tomato, grain, and scallion. Grain-heavy salads that pretend to be tabbouleh are simply an insult to the real thing. That being said, you can add diced hot chile pepper if you like it spicy, and a bit of lemon zest will give your tabbouleh extra tang. For the very best results, use locally grown, seasonal ingredients—an essential part of Lebanese cooking. All over Beirut, you can spot herbs and vegetables growing on balconies in old tin cans; families use homegrown ingredients with great pride.

4–5 bunches flat-leaf parsley

½ bunch mint, leaves stripped

¼ cup (50 g) fine bulgur

Juice of 1–2 lemons

½ cup (120 ml) extra-virgin olive oil, or to taste

1 lb (450 g) firm, ripe, bright red tomatoes, finely chopped, liquid reserved

3–4 scallions, trimmed

1 teaspoon salt, or to taste

½ teaspoon ground allspice

Romaine hearts, cabbage leaves, or fresh grape leaves, to serve

Prepare the parsley: Pick through the bunches to remove any spoiled stalks. Wash the parsley thoroughly under cold running water and shake off the excess water. Tie the bunches of stalks as you would a bouquet of flowers and leave them to dry in a colander, stalk side down, while you work on the other ingredients. If the stalks are not completely dry, spin them in a salad spinner to dry thoroughly before chopping. If the stalks are still wet, it will result in mushy tabbouleh. To finely chop the parsley, hold the bunch in one hand and chop with the other using a sharp knife. Start chopping from the stalk end and move up. You can never get good results using a food processor to chop parsley for tabbouleh.

Finely chop the mint, being careful not to over-handle the leaves, since they can bruise easily. Set aside.

Briefly rinse the bulgur under cold running water and drain well. Place it in a large mixing bowl and pour in the lemon juice, olive oil, and chopped tomatoes, along with any liquid left on the chopping board. Set aside for 5 to 10 minutes, until the liquid has been absorbed and the bulgur has softened.

Finely chop the scallions, and place them in a small bowl. Mix in 1 teaspoon of salt (this will reduce their sharpness), and the allspice.

Return to your bulgur. Using your hands—the Lebanese way—mix the bulgur and tomatoes together. Then mix in the scallions, followed by the chopped parsley and mint. Taste and add more salt, lemon juice, or olive oil to your liking. Serve with young leaves of romaine lettuce, cabbage, or fresh grape leaves, which you can use to scoop the tabbouleh into your mouth.

# Peasant Salad

## *Fattoush*

You can make this salad with whatever fresh local produce you can find. That's the beauty of it! You just need some good quality sumac (made from 100% sumac berries) and some Arabic bread, and your *fattoush* will burst with flavors. Bread that has been lying around a bit too long is perfect for frying or toasting and it is an essential part of this recipe. In our culture, throwing away bread is *haram*—a sacrilege, so we have a number of recipes that find delicious ways to use day-old bread. Sumac and pomegranate molasses can be found in Middle Eastern grocery stores and well-stocked supermarkets.

1 head romaine lettuce, chopped

2 bunches purslane (or use arugula)

3–4 cups (115 g) baby arugula

1 bunch flat-leaf parsley, chopped

½ bunch mint, leaves stripped

4 Lebanese cucumbers, sliced

3–4 tomatoes, cut into wedges

5–6 radishes, sliced

1 green bell pepper, chopped

1 red bell pepper, chopped

1 medium onion, sliced

3 scallions, finely chopped (optional)

### GARNISH

1–2 loaves Arabic bread (p. 28),
  cut into squares or thin strips

Vegetable oil, for frying (optional)

1–2 tablespoons ground sumac

### DRESSING

1–2 garlic cloves

Juice of ½ lemon

¼ cup (60 ml) pomegranate molasses
  (or use balsamic vinegar)

½ cup (120 ml) extra-virgin olive oil

Salt

Put the lettuce in a large salad bowl (the prettiest and largest bowl you have). Strip the purslane leaves and add them to the bowl, along with the rest of the salad ingredients (or experiment with what you have available!). This is where your senses will start to tingle.

Bake, grill, or deep-fry the pieces of bread. Deep-frying is traditional—you can't beat that taste! Set aside.

To make the dressing, crush the garlic to a paste with a pinch of salt in a mortar and pestle. Add the lemon juice, pomegranate molasses, and finally, the extra-virgin olive oil. Taste and add more salt, if needed.

Just before serving, pour the dressing onto the salad, sprinkle with sumac, and toss. Add the bread and toss again. Serve immediately or the bread will get soggy.

# Purslane, Tomato, and Cucumber Salad

*Salatet Baqleh ma' Banadoura wa Khyar*

Purslane is a well-loved leafy green that grows wild all over Lebanon and in many other places around the world. In some countries it is considered a weed, but don't let this discourage you. It is a highly nutritious plant loaded with antioxidants, minerals, and omega-3 fatty acids. Delicious cooked or raw, it is one of the main ingredients in *Fattoush* (Peasant salad, p. 16), used as a stuffing for small turnovers like *fatayer* (see p. 44), and cooked in another local dish where it is blended with garlicky yogurt. You will find purslane in farmers' markets or maybe even growing wild in your garden. Prepare this salad at the last minute using the freshest ingredients.

2 bunches purslane (or use baby arugula or watercress)

4–5 medium tomatoes, quartered

2–3 Lebanese or Persian cucumbers, sliced

2–3 scallions, or 1 small onion, trimmed and finely chopped

1 tablespoon ground sumac

**DRESSING**

1 garlic clove

Juice of 1 lemon

½ cup (120 ml) extra-virgin olive oil

Salt

Wash the purslane and drain well in a colander or salad spinner. Strip the leaves from the stalks, taking extra care—the leaves bruise easily. Discard the stalks. Place the leaves in a serving bowl.

To make the dressing, crush the garlic to a paste with a pinch of salt in a mortar and pestle. Add the lemon juice, olive oil, and more salt to taste. Set aside.

Add the tomatoes, cucumbers, and scallions to the serving bowl. Sprinkle with the sumac, and pour the dressing over the salad. Toss to mix and serve immediately.

# Red Lentil Salad with Pomegranate Molasses

## *Salatet Addas wa Dibs Rumman*

I got this tangy salad recipe from a good friend, Aline Kamakian, who owns and operates two Armenian restaurants in Beirut. She is a redhead and crazy about food and life. Sound familiar? When she opened her second restaurant, Batchig, I brought my father there for lunch for his birthday. We enjoyed an assortment of dishes, but the lentil salad left a huge impression on both of us. I immediately contacted Aline to ask for the recipe. The next day, I received her response. Generosity is crucial in this business, not only with food, but with knowledge.

Use tiny whole brown lentils, not the orange split kind, which lose their shape fast during cooking. The recipe calls for lots of lemon juice, which gives this salad its kick. Serve it as a light vegetarian meal or as an accompaniment to grilled meat, poultry, or fish dishes.

1¼ cups (250 g) small brown lentils
½ teaspoon ground allspice
¼ teaspoon freshly ground
    black pepper
½ teaspoon ground cumin
1 teaspoon Aleppo pepper
    or cayenne
2 medium tomatoes, finely
    chopped
1 small onion, or 2–3 scallions,
    finely chopped
1 small bunch cilantro, leaves
    finely chopped

**DRESSING**
1½ teaspoons salt
¼ cup (60 ml) pomegranate
    molasses
1 cup (240 ml) freshly squeezed
    lemon juice
2 tablespoons extra-virgin olive oil

Spread the lentils on a tray and pick through them to remove any small stones or impurities. Rinse under cold running water and drain.

Place the lentils in a pot with enough water to cover them. Bring to a boil, then reduce the heat and simmer for 20 to 25 minutes until tender but still holding their shape. Drain the lentils and rinse them under cold running water. Drain well and put them in a large serving bowl. Set aside to cool completely.

Meanwhile, whisk together the ingredients for the dressing and set aside.

Once the lentils are cool, add the spices, tomatoes, onion or scallions, and cilantro and toss well. Gently mix in the dressing, taste for seasoning, and serve, or cover and refrigerate until ready to serve.

# Beet Salad with Purslane, Feta, and Walnuts

## *Salatet Shamandar ma' Baqleh, Feta wa Joz*

Fuchsia is one of my favorite colors. Fuchsia-colored food is even better. Earthy and vibrant, this fall salad is quick to make and tastes great, with its combination of beets, walnuts, and creamy feta (get the best quality you can find). A dressing made with thick, tangy pomegranate molasses adds the perfect sweet and sour note. Look for pomegranate molasses in Middle Eastern grocery stores and well-stocked supermarkets (I like Cortas brand).

3 large red beets

½ cup (50 g) walnuts, coarsely chopped (or use pistachios)

1 bunch purslane (or use baby arugula or watercress)

2 scallions, trimmed and finely chopped

3½ oz (100 g) feta cheese, cubed

**DRESSING**

¼ cup (60 ml) freshly squeezed lemon juice

1 tablespoon pomegranate molasses

½ cup (120 ml) extra-virgin olive oil

1 teaspoon salt

Preheat the oven to 350°F (180°C). Individually wrap each beet in foil and place on a nonstick baking pan. Roast for 45 minutes, or until just tender. Alternatively, you can boil them for 30 minutes or until easily pierced with a fork. Wearing gloves to protect your hands and nails, peel the beets while they are still warm and cut them into ½ in (1 cm) cubes. Set aside in the refrigerator.

In a dry frying pan, toast the walnuts until they are slightly browned. Set aside to cool.

Whisk together the dressing ingredients and set aside.

When you are ready to serve, combine the greens and scallions in a large serving bowl, and toss. Mix in the beets, walnuts, and feta, then pour over the dressing. Serve immediately, or the beets will color the rest of the ingredients. Serve cold or at room temperature.

# BREADS & SAVORY PASTRIES

# BREADS & SAVORY PASTRIES

*Khubz wa Mu'ajjanat*

Dough has always been an obsession of mine—and still is. I bake sourdough bread every week for my family. I built a starter years ago and hope to keep it alive for a very long time. Perhaps one day when my children are ready, they will make use of it to bake their own.

My baking adventure started when I was a young mother with three young children. I felt the need to let off some steam once in a while. I would take refuge in the kitchen and make dough to relax, as one would do a yoga session. As the adage goes, "Bread is more than just flour, water, and salt. It needs nurturing and care." The house would smell divine and the family would rejoice to eat fresh bread. My son, then just starting middle school, when asked what his mother did for a living would say, "*Ma maman est une boulangère*"—My mother is a baker. Later in life, he would go on to learn the secrets of bread making professionally, training at the Pozzoli bakery in Lyon, France.

When my youngest daughter started preschool, I decided to train in restaurant kitchens in Beirut. I felt the urge to go back to a professional kitchen where one experiences the joy of cooking and the adrenaline of serving diners. I was lucky to be welcomed into a number of restaurants: French, Italian, and Lebanese. The experience I gained in the Abdel Wahab Restaurant in Beirut remains an important stepping stone in my pursuit of understanding our local food heritage. I went through the different sections of the kitchen and learned techniques to cook Lebanese food professionally. I was most at ease in a small room where fresh Arabic bread and assortments of savory pastries were cooked in a hot oven every day. These were served to diners alongside a wide selection of offerings—mainly mezze. I would spend hours with Mohammad, the baker, discussing the techniques of bread making.

Pizza has also always fascinated me, especially the history behind this popular Italian street food. I had dreams of going to Italy and delving deeper into the subject. I wanted to meet bakers, bake with them, and take photos. One always thinks that the grass is greener on the other side. One day, after deep reflection, I decided to take this journey in my own country. I would start by visiting bakers all around Lebanon in search of *man'oushé* (our traditional topped flatbread) and all its derivatives. Two hundred and fifty bakeries later, with lots of adventures and hard work, my first book was published: *Man'oushé: Inside the Lebanese Street Corner Bakery*. The book became very popular. When you mention *man'oushé* to Lebanese people, it automatically brings them joyful memories, putting a smile on their faces. Walking on the streets of Beirut, the smell of *za'atar* is imminent. One need only follow the scent to arrive at the nearest neighborhood bakery. Across the country, despite our ethnic differences, this iconic street food is our common denominator.

**Left:** Martyrs' Monument in downtown Beirut, built by Mazzacurati, an Italian sculptor, in honor of a cross-confessional group of Lebanese patriots in 1916 who opposed Turkish rule. Today protesters gather here to demonstrate for change in the future of Lebanon.

# Arabic Bread

## *Khubz Arabi*

Arabic bread plays an essential role in every meal in our culture. We often use it instead of forks and knives, scooping tasty morsels into our mouths. We use it to wipe our plates clean of cooking juices, and to dip into a variety of mezze dishes. Grilled meats and vegetables are often served tucked in a pocket of Arabic bread; the bottom layer soaks up the juices, while the top layer keeps the food warm. The bread is lifted as one would lift a veil to showcase its contents. Often, families will buy fresh bread and separate the layers—the whiter top part is used to accompany a meal, and the lower red part, which is thicker, is used to make sandwiches. This recipe also forms the base of the topped flatbread recipes on pp. 31, 34, 35, and 36.

In the Arab world, bread is seen as sacred, a gift from God. There are strict rules to follow, which include breaking the bread with your hands. If one uses a knife, it is as if one is raising a sword against God. Only in restaurants do they use scissors to cut the bread. Should a piece of bread accidentally fall on the ground, it is picked up immediately and pressed to the lips and forehead as a sign of respect. Leftover bread is never thrown away. It is toasted or fried and used as a garnish for soups, or as one of the central ingredients in *Fattoush* (Peasant Salad, p. 16) and *fatteh* dishes (see p. 66). Bread is all about sharing and conviviality, making a meal a communal affair. We often use the expression "*fi baynatna khubz wa meleh*," which translates to "There is bread and salt between us," signifying a strong bond.

1 teaspoon (3 g) active-dry yeast

1¼ cups (300 ml) lukewarm water
 (body temperature is best)

3½ cups (420 g) all-purpose flour
 (or 2⅔ cups/300 g wholewheat
 flour plus 1 cup/120 g
 all-purpose flour), plus
 extra for dusting

1 teaspoon salt for bread,
 2 teaspoons for flatbread bases

1 teaspoon sugar for bread,
 1 tablespoon for flatbread bases

1 tablespoon extra-virgin olive oil,
 plus extra for greasing

Dissolve the yeast in the water and set aside for a couple of minutes until frothy. In a mixing bowl, sift the flour(s) and salt together and stir in the sugar (it is important to mix the dry ingredients first). Stir 1 tablespoon of the olive oil into the yeast mixture and pour it into a large mixing bowl or the bowl of a stand mixer. Gradually beat the flour into the yeast mixture until it starts to come together into a soft dough (if using whole wheat flour, you may need to add a little more water, a tablespoon at a time, to achieve this).

To knead by hand, tip the dough out onto a lightly floured surface and knead the dough for 5 to 10 minutes until smooth and elastic. Alternatively, knead for 3 minutes in a stand mixer, or for 1 minute in a food processor, starting at a low speed, then gradually turning up the speed. Always stay close to your machine while it is running.

Transfer the dough to a large bowl dusted with flour or greased with 1 tablespoon of olive oil. Cover the bowl with a damp dish towel and leave to rise in a warm place free of drafts for 1½ to 2 hours, or until doubled in size.

Punch down the dough. On a floured surface, form the dough into a log. Pinch off the dough to form equal pieces, (6 to 8 for bread, depending on how thin you like it; 4 for flatbread bases). Using a rolling pin, roll out each ball of dough into a circle about 10 in (25 cm) in diameter. Cover again with the dish towel and set aside for 10 minutes.

Use the prepared dough in flatbread recipes or bake your breads using the following method: Place a baking stone or upturned baking pan on the bottom shelf of your oven and preheat to 425°F (220°C). Working in batches, place the circles of dough directly on the baking pan or stone and bake for 3 to 5 minutes, watching carefully so they don't burn. Your bread is ready when a hollow pocket has formed and the bread is slightly browned on the edges and on the top.

Arabic bread is best eaten hot out of the oven because it tends to dry out quickly. If you want to store the bread for later consumption, allow it to cool, flatten, then store in sealed plastic bags in the refrigerator or freezer.

MAKES 4

# Wild Thyme Flatbread

*Man'oushé bi Za'atar*

*Man'oushé*, flatbread topped with *za'atar* and olive oil, cheese, or a variety of other toppings, is our most beloved street food. It is the food of the rich and poor alike. It has a reserved place on the country's breakfast table and a unique ability to be worked into every meal of the day.

Every street corner in Lebanon has a small bakery and community oven, *fern*, that caters to the neighborhood. In a tradition that originated before households had their own ovens, families across Lebanon bring their own *man'oushé* toppings to the *fern*, placing their trust in the baker by saying "*a zawak*," meaning make it the way you see fit. All across Lebanon, the *nesween el fern*, "the women of the bakery" gather in the morning to wait for their flatbread to be baked, drinking coffee and sharing worries, joys, complaints, and gossip.

There are many ways to cook your *man'oushé*—choose the method that best fits your lifestyle.

1 recipe flatbread bases (p. 28)

½ cup (60 g) *za'atar* (see Note)

½ cup (120 ml) extra-virgin olive oil (or a mixture of olive oil and vegetable oil)

**TO SERVE (OPTIONAL)**

Labneh (Thick Strained Yogurt, p. 94)

Mint leaves

Sliced cucumbers

Sliced tomatoes

Pickles

Olives

Ready your flatbread bases. In a small bowl, stir the *za'atar* with the oil until evenly mixed. Using the back of a spoon, spread the mixture over the prepared dough, leaving about ½ in (1 cm) of exposed dough at the edges. For more even distribution, use your fingertips.

If you are oven-baking: Place a baking stone or upturned baking pan on the bottom shelf of your oven and preheat to 400°F (200°C). Working in batches if necessary, place the dough rounds directly on the upturned baking pan or baking stone and bake for 7 to 10 minutes, until the dough is cooked and the edges are slightly golden, watching carefully so they don't burn.

Alternatively, use a cast-iron crepe pan, griddle, or *saj* (convex disc pan): Heat your pan over high heat. Place a dough round in the pan and heat until small bubbles form; then lower the heat and spread on the topping. Cook until the bottom is slightly golden and the edges are crisp, 3 to 5 minutes, depending on the heat source. Lightly spray the cooking surface with water between batches and wipe away any debris.

Serve the flatbread hot with a spoonful of labneh, mint leaves, cucumbers, tomatoes, pickles, and olives as desired.

**Note** Za'atar is a spice mixture made predominantly from the herb of the same name that grows wild throughout the Levant (sometimes called wild thyme or Lebanese oregano). The herb is dried and crumbled with sumac, salt, sesame seeds, and sometimes other spices or nuts depending on the region or family tradition. You can buy it in Middle Eastern grocery stores or well-stocked supermarkets.

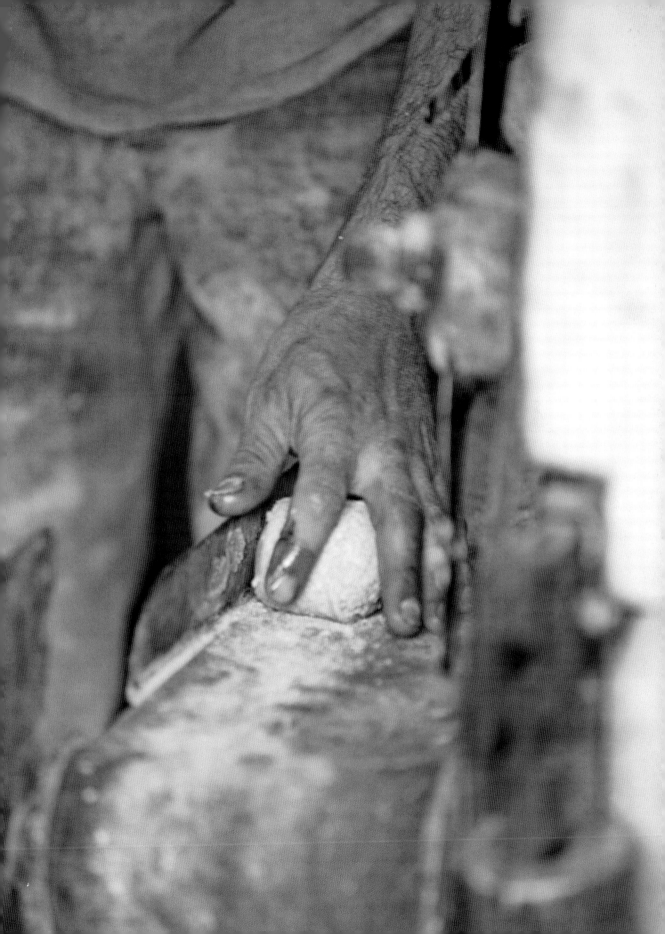

# Cheese Flatbread

## *Man'oushé bi Jibneh*

*Man'oushé bi jibneh* (cheese) is the most popular pie ordered in the Lebanese street-corner bakery, after *Man'oushé bi Za'atar* (Wild Thyme Flatbread, p. 31). It is made with *'Akkawi* cheese, a mild, salty white brine cheese that melts in your mouth. It is simple comfort food that hits the spot every time. When I was pregnant with my first child, I would stop at the same bakery on the coastal highway every single day on my way to work to eat *man'oushé bi jibneh*, not skipping one day. It would give me the energy I needed to get through the day. Could this have been an early precursor to writing my first book on the subject years later? Or perhaps it is why my son, Albert, grew up to pursue a culinary career... Who knows!

1 recipe flatbread bases (p. 28)

4 cups (500 g) grated *'Akkawi* cheese or firm mozzarella

4 tablespoons vegetable oil or melted butter (optional)

Pinch dried mint, sesame seeds, nigella seeds, ground coriander or Aleppo pepper, to serve

Ready your flatbread bases. *'Akkawi* cheese is typically very salty. To reduce the salt content, soak the grated cheese in water overnight, changing the water two or three times, if possible. If time does not permit, soak the grated cheese for a couple of hours, then run cold water over the cheese in a colander. Drain very well before using. (No need to do this if using firm mozzarella.)

If you are oven-baking: Place a baking stone or upturned baking pan on the bottom shelf of your oven and preheat to 400°F (200°C). Sprinkle the cheese evenly on the prepared dough, leaving about ½ in (1 cm) of exposed dough at the edges. You may sprinkle tablespoon of vegetable oil or butter on top, for flavor and elasticity. Working in batches if necessary, place the dough rounds directly on the upturned baking pan or baking stone and bake for 7 to 10 minutes, until the dough is cooked and the cheese is slightly golden, watching carefully to make sure it does not burn.

Alternatively, preheat a cast-iron crepe pan, griddle, or *saj* (convex disc pan), over high heat. Place a dough round on the pan and heat until small bubbles form; then lower the heat and pile the cheese the middle of the dough for about 30 second to melt it, before spreading it evenly over the dough. This method will prevent the cheese from running onto your cooking surface. Cook until the bottom is slightly golden and the edges are crisp, 3 to 5 minutes. Lightly spray the cooking surface with water between batches and wipe away any debris.

Garnish the flatbread with a sprinkle of dried mint, sesame seeds, nigella seeds, ground coriander, or Aleppo pepper and serve hot.

# Spicy Red Pepper Flatbread

*Man'oushé bi Flayfleh Harra*

Hot and spicy, this pie is not for the faint-hearted! If you want to live the full experience, start by making your own red pepper paste from scratch (p. 200) then use it to make this delicious topped flatbread. Preserving the abundance of the season is an important part of our food culture. When you make your own preserves, you feel the difference and enjoy every bite all the more.

This is the basic recipe, but you can play around with it until you find your favorite combination: Add one finely chopped tomato to the mixture, or omit the walnuts and top the mixture with a thick layer of grated cheese. Sprinkle the top with nigella seeds to add subtle flavor and dramatic visual contrast to this gorgeous flaming red pie.

1 recipe flatbread bases (p. 28)

2 medium onions, finely chopped

¼ cup (60 g) red pepper paste (p. 200)

1 cup (100 g) walnuts, coarsely chopped

1 cup (240 ml) extra-virgin olive oil

½ teaspoon ground cumin

4 tablespoons nigella seeds (optional)

Ready your flatbread bases. In a bowl, mix the onions, red pepper paste, walnuts, olive oil, and cumin.

If you are oven-baking: Place a baking stone or upturned baking pan on the bottom shelf of your oven and preheat to 400°F (200°C). Using the back of a spoon, spread the mixture over the prepared dough, leaving about ½ in (1 cm) of exposed dough at the edges. Top with the nigella seeds, if using. Working in batches if necessary, place the dough rounds directly on the upturned baking pan or baking stone and bake for 7 to 10 minutes until the edges are slightly golden, watching carefully so they don't burn.

Alternatively, use a cast-iron crepe pan, griddle, or convex disc (*saj*), preheat over high heat. Heat the dough rounds until small bubbles form; then lower the heat, spread on the topping, and sprinkle with nigella seeds, if using. Cook until the bottom is slightly golden and the edges are crisp, 3 to 5 minutes. Lightly spray the cooking surface with water between batches and wipe away any debris.

Serve the flatbread hot.

# Kishk Flatbread

## *Man'oushé bi Kishk*

Made into a smooth paste and baked onto flatbread, *kishk*, a fine powder made from dried fermented cracked wheat and yogurt (see p. 8), is taken to another level. The quality of the *kishk* is of utmost importance to get good results. People from Beirut will get their yearly supply from villagers who make *kishk* every year, mostly in the fall when the weather is still warm and the wheat has been harvested. Families will often make their own *kishk* topping mixture and bring it to the local bakery to bake onto flatbread. Because of the demand for *kishk* pies recently, bakers all over Lebanon have added this variety to their menus.

1 recipe flatbread bases (p. 28)

½ cup (50 g) *kishk*

2 medium tomatoes, finely chopped

1 medium onion, finely chopped or grated

1 cup (100 g) walnuts, coarsely chopped (optional)

1 tablespoon red pepper paste (p. 200)

1 teaspoon tomato paste

½ cup (120 ml) extra-virgin olive oil

4 tablespoons sesame seeds (optional)

Ready your flatbread bases. In a bowl, mix the *kishk* with the tomatoes, onion, walnuts (if using), red pepper paste, tomato paste, and olive oil. You may need to add some water to loosen the mixture to a sauce-like consistency. Alternatively, sauté the onion with red pepper paste, tomato paste, and the fresh tomatoes in a small frying pan, then add the mixture to the *kishk* and walnuts (if using) with olive oil.

Preheat the oven to 400°F (200°C). Using the back of a spoon spread the mixture over the prepared dough, leaving about ½ in (1cm) of exposed dough at the edges. Top with sesame seeds, if using. Bake for 7 to 10 minutes on the bottom shelf until the edges are slightly golden, watching carefully so they don't burn.

Alternatively, use a cast-iron crepe pan, griddle, or convex disc (*saj*), preheat over high heat. Heat the dough until small bubbles form; then lower the heat and spread on the topping and top with sesame seeds, if using. Cook until the bottom is slightly golden and the edges are crisp, about 3 to 5 minutes, depending on the heat source. Lightly spray the cooking surface with water between batches and wipe away any debris.

Serve the flatbread hot.

# Armenian Meat Flatbread

## Lahm bi 'Ajeen Armani

It is not uncommon to find a butcher and bakery on the same street. The baker will conveniently get the finest cuts needed to make *lahm bi 'ajeen*, flatbread topped with a spiced ground meat mixture. The freshest ingredients are carefully chosen early in the morning according to the customers' daily demands. The best meat pies in Lebanon are made by the Armenian community, mostly in Bourj Hamoud north-east of Beirut, and in Anjar in the Bekaa Valley, where there is a large Armenian population. My paternal grandmother was Armenian, and I have always been fascinated with Armenian food culture and flavors. I guess it's in the blood—the yearning for it. You can make these in two sizes.

## DOUGH

1 teaspoon (3 g) active-dry yeast

1¼ cups (300 ml) lukewarm water
  (body temperature is best)

3½ cups (420 g) all-purpose flour,
  plus extra for dusting

2 teaspoons salt

## TOPPING

2 medium onions

4 large or 6 medium tomatoes

4 to 5 garlic cloves

½ green bell pepper

½ bunch flat-leaf parsley, finely
  chopped by hand

8 oz (250 g) finely ground beef or
  lamb with 25% fat for the best
  flavor (you can pulse ground meat
  in a food processor to achieve a
  find grind)

1 teaspoon red pepper paste
  (p. 200), or to taste

½ teaspoon ground allspice

*Continued on next page*

Dissolve the yeast in the water and set aside for a couple of minutes. In a mixing bowl, sift the flour and salt together and stir in the sugar (it is important to mix the dry ingredients first). Stir 1 tablespoon of the olive oil into the yeast mixture and pour it into a large mixing bowl or the bowl of a stand mixer. Gradually beat the flour into the yeast mixture until it starts to come together into a soft dough.

To knead by hand, dip the dough out onto a lightly floured surface and knead the dough for 5 to 10 minutes until smooth and elastic. Alternatively, knead for 3 minutes in a stand mixer, or for 1 minute in a food processor, starting at a low speed, then gradually turning up the speed. Always stay close to your machine while it is running.

Transfer the dough to a large bowl dusted with flour or greased with 1 tablespoon of olive oil. Cover the bowl with a damp dish towel and leave to rise in a warm place free of drafts for 1½ to 2 hours, or until doubled in size.

Punch down the dough. On a floured surface, form the dough into a log. Divide the dough into 16 equal pieces (for larger pies) or 24 equal pieces (for smaller pies). Roll each piece out to paper-thin rounds; 8 in (20 cm) in diameter for large pies, or 5 in (12 cm) for small ones. Cover again with the dish towel and set aside for 10 minutes.

Make the topping: Quarter the onions and tomatoes and place them in the bowl of a food processor. Add the garlic and bell pepper and pulse until evenly finely chopped. Alternatively, finely chop them by hand.

In a mixing bowl, combine the ground meat, red pepper paste, allspice, salt, pepper, and pine nuts, if using. Mix the ground vegetables and parsley into the meat and knead with your hands to create an even, dough-like

1½ teaspoons salt

Pinch freshly ground black pepper

½ cup (70 g) pine nuts (optional)

Lemon wedges, to serve

Pinch Aleppo pepper or cayenne, to serve

consistency. Transfer the mixture to a colander to drain excess liquid, and divide the mixture into 16 or 24 pieces (according to how many dough rounds you have).

If you are oven-baking: Preheat the oven to 400°F (200°C). Spread the meat mixture over the whole surface of the prepared dough (the meat will shrink during cooking). Working in batches if necessary, place the dough rounds directly on the upturned baking pan or baking stone and bake for 5 to 7 minutes, until the meat and dough are cooked and the edges are slightly golden, watching carefully so they don't burn.

Alternatively, use a cast-iron crepe pan, griddle, or *saj* (convex disc pan), preheat over high heat. Place a dough round on the pan and heat until small bubbles form; then spread the meat over the whole surface of the dough. Turn down the heat to low (to ensure the meat cooks evenly), and cook until the bottom is slightly golden, the edges are crisp, and the meat is cooked, about 5 minutes. Lightly spray the cooking surface with water between batches and wipe away any debris.

Serve the pies hot with a squeeze of lemon juice or a pinch of red pepper.

# Meat Crescents

## *Sambousek*

These small meat-filled pastries are fun for the whole family to make and bake. Ask your children to roll out the dough and cut out circles using a pastry cutter or glass. It will keep them happily occupied for a while. There is also a cheese variation where the meat stuffing is replaced with a mixture of cheese, onion, and parsley. You can fry or bake *sambousek* in the oven, the latter being the lighter option. I often make a big batch and, once the crescents are formed, freeze them, first on a tray, before transferring them to freezer bags. Then it is easy to bake or fry them at the last moment when you have hungry unexpected guests. They make a great snack or appetizer to serve with cold drinks.

## DOUGH

3½ cups (420 g) all-purpose flour, plus extra for dusting

1½ teaspoons salt

1 teaspoon sugar

½ cup (120 ml) vegetable oil (or a mixture of oil and melted butter), plus extra for brushing

1½ cups (350 ml) lukewarm water

## STUFFING

2 tablespoons vegetable oil

1 large onion, finely chopped

½ cup (70 g) pine nuts

8 oz (250 g) ground beef or lamb with 25% fat for the best flavor

½ teaspoon salt

½ teaspoon ground allspice

¼ teaspoon ground cinnamon

Pinch freshly ground black pepper

1 tablespoon pomegranate molasses

Vegetable oil, for frying

Prepare the dough: Start by sifting the flour and salt together into a large mixing bowl. Stir in the sugar. Pour in the oil, mixing with your fingers. Gradually mix in the water and then knead with your fingers until it comes together into a soft dough. Tip the dough onto a lightly floured surface and knead for 3 to 5 minutes, just until smooth and elastic. Don't overwork the dough or it won't be flaky. Set aside in a bowl covered with a damp kitchen towel.

To make the stuffing, start by heating the oil in a deep frying pan over medium heat. Add the onion and sauté for 2 minutes. Add the pine nuts. When the onion is translucent, add the beef or lamb. Season with the spices and then add the pomegranate molasses. Cook for 8 to 10 minutes, breaking the meat up with your spoon. When the meat is cooked, remove from heat and set aside.

On a lightly floured surface, use a rolling pin to roll the dough out as evenly and thinly as possible (ideally about 3 mm thick). Cut out 3 in (8 cm) circles using a pastry cutter or the top of a glass. Top each circle with 1 tablespoon of stuffing. Fold in half to cover the stuffing and press the edges together to seal into a semicircle. Next, the tricky part: Crimp the edges with your fingers, making tight overlapping folds, or use a fork to seal the edges. This gives your pastries the traditional look, but you can skip this step if you prefer.

At this stage you can freeze them (to cook, remove from the freezer and continue as below).

Let them stand for 30 minutes before cooking according to one of the following methods.

Pour vegetable oil into a large pot or deep-fryer to a depth of 2 in (5 cm). Heat until the oil reaches a temperature of 350°F (180°C), or until small bubbles gather around a small piece of bread dropped into the oil. Fry the *sambousek*, in small batches, for 3 to 5 minutes, until evenly golden. Lift them out of the pot with tongs, shake off the oil, and transfer to paper towels or a steel colander to drain.

To oven bake, preheat your oven to 350°F (180°C) and lightly oil 2 large baking pans (you may need to bake in batches). Space the *sambousek* out on the pans, lightly brush the tops with oil, and bake for 20 minutes, or until golden brown.

Serve at room temperature.

# Spinach Turnovers
## *Fatayer Sbenegh*

Think of *fatayer* as delicious greens comfortably baked into a parcel of bread. Usually made bite-size, they fall into the category of *mu'ajjanat*—small savory pastries. Once you eat one, you simply can't stop. This is the basic recipe—by all means be creative; you can add crushed walnuts, raisins, pine nuts, or some cheese (like *'Akkawi* or feta) to the stuffing. Or replace the spinach with other greens, like sorrel, dandelion greens, chard, or purslane. These small ones freeze well, or you can make larger sized turnovers if you prefer (see Variation).

### DOUGH

3½ cups (420 g) all-purpose flour,
  plus extra for dusting
1 teaspoon sugar
1½ teaspoons salt
½ cup (120 ml) vegetable oil,
  plus extra for brushing
1½ cup (350 ml) lukewarm water

### STUFFING

1 lb (450 g) spinach leaves (from
  a 4½ lb/2 kg bunch of spinach)
1 tablespoon salt, plus a pinch
1 onion, finely chopped
¼ teaspoon freshly ground
  black pepper
1 medium tomato, finely chopped
2 tablespoons ground sumac
Juice of 1 lemon
½ cup (120 ml) extra-virgin olive oil

Prepare the dough: Sift the flour into a large mixing bowl and stir in the sugar and salt. Pour in the oil, mixing with your fingers. Gradually mix in the water until it comes together. Tip the dough onto a lightly floured surface and knead for 3 to 5 minutes until smooth and elastic. Don't overwork the dough or it won't be flaky. Set aside in a bowl covered with a damp kitchen towel.

Carefully rinse the spinach leaves in cold water. Drain and dry well. Coarsely chop the leaves. Add the salt and gently rub the salt and spinach together. This will help draw out any excess water. Drain the spinach again.

Place the onion in a large mixing bowl and sprinkle with a pinch of salt and pepper. Using your hands (wearing gloves if your hands are sensitive), rub them together to soften the onions and squeeze out excess moisture. Add the spinach, tomato, sumac, lemon juice, and olive oil. Mix well with your hands.

Lightly oil two large baking sheets. On a floured surface, form the dough into a log and divide it into 4 equal balls. Flatten each ball with your palm, then use a rolling pin to roll out as evenly and thinly as possible (ideally about 3 mm). Cut out 3 in (8 cm) circles using a pastry cutter or the top of a glass. Drop a generous tablespoon of the spinach mixture in the center of each circle. Fold the edges of the dough over the filling in thirds and firmly pinch the edges together to form a triangular parcel. Space the formed turnovers out on your baking sheets. At this stage you can freeze them (to cook, remove from the freezer and continue as below).

Preheat the oven to 350°F (180°C). Brush the tops of the turnovers with oil and let stand for 30 minutes. Bake for 20 minutes until golden brown and cooked. Serve warm or at room temperature.

**Variation** To make large *fatayer*, roll the dough into 4 to 6 thin rounds. Divide the stuffing accordingly. Adjust the baking time to 7 to 10 minutes.

# Cheese Rolls

*Rakakat Jibneh*

These pastry-wrapped cheese rolls are delicious and will be eaten up in a matter of seconds. They are easy to make too; the perfect party food. The crunchy phyllo (paper-thin sheets of unleavened pastry) makes the rolls taste light even though they are fried. I also make a version using shredded mozzarella cheese topped with a slice of *basterma* (air-dried cured beef), inspired by innovative versions I have tried from new local restaurants. It is popular nowadays to revisit and adapt traditional Lebanese recipes, but always using seasonal, local ingredients. I am in favor of moving forward, but always with great respect for our culinary heritage.

1 lb (450 g) feta cheese, crumbled (or use goat cheese)

1 small onion, finely chopped

1 bunch flat-leaf parsley, finely chopped

Pinch Aleppo pepper or cayenne

Salt and freshly ground black pepper

1 lb (450 g) package phyllo pastry sheets, thawed overnight in the refrigerator

1 large egg

Vegetable oil, for deep-frying

In a large mixing bowl, mix together the feta, onion, and parsley. Season with Aleppo pepper, black pepper, and salt, if needed.

Before you begin, bring the phyllo pastry to room temperature without opening. Your hands should be dry when you start handling the dough. Remove the packaging and carefully unroll the sheets. Cut into squares about 5 in (12 cm). Cover the pastry with a sheet of wax paper, then with a damp kitchen towel to keep it moist while you work; it tends to dry very quickly. Each time you remove a sheet, cover the rest.

Make an egg wash: In a small bowl, mix the egg with 1 tablespoon of water and use a fork to combine.

Lay a sheet of the dough flat on your work surface. Spread 1 tablespoon of the filling horizontally along one end, 1 in (2 cm) from the edge closest to you. Fold in the sides, then fold the bottom edge up over the filling and gently press. Roll up the pastry dough as you would a cigar, then brush the edges with egg wash to seal. Set on a plate, seam side down. Repeat with remaining dough and cheese mixture.

Pour vegetable oil into a large pot or deep-fryer to a depth of 2 in (5 cm). Heat until the oil reaches a temperature of 350°F (180°C), or until small bubbles gather around a small piece of bread dropped into the oil. Working in batches, fry the rolls for about 2 minutes, until golden brown and crisp on all sides. Using a slotted spoon, transfer to a plate or steel colander lined with paper towels to drain excess oil. Serve immediately.

# MEZZE

# MEZZE

If a single image could define our unique food culture and heritage, it would certainly depict an oversized table groaning with small, colorful plates of food, the clanging of glasses and plates surrounded by happy people caught in the act of socializing and sharing a meal. Mezze is a feast for the eyes as well as for the palate: a ritual displaying abundance, generosity, and variety. We connect to each other as plates are passed and conversations rise and fall. Dishes can be served in a casual manner, be it in the shade of an old tree in the mountains, at a quaint seaside eatery, in a vibrant street or market, or simply in the comfort of homes. One shares good food, drinks, and pleasant conversation with family and friends. Preparing the mezze, therefore, is more important than ever as an element of our social fabric.

I was raised knowing that food was my family's livelihood. Our convivial family restaurant in Florida served Lebanese mezze daily, and these plates of delicious food acted as little ambassadors of the faraway land we called home. The ritual of serving mezze, hot and cold dishes of varying texture, flavor, and aroma, was a spectacular showcase of the riches our native land had to offer. Our guests were endlessly surprised and delighted, begging to know the ingredients and origins of the food. I recall one customer gifting me a collection of cassettes (remember this was the '80s) of Fairuz in recognition of our good food and hospitality.

In a typical Lebanese restaurant, where mezze is the main attraction, menus are seldom offered to customers to take their orders. Instead, the head waiter will arrive to the table with a small notebook to name all the dishes, one by one. Diners will decide after hearing each suggestion if they are interested in ordering the dish. Discussions follow on the main specialties of the restaurant, as these differ regionally. Coastal restaurants put more emphasis on seafood; whereas in the mountain the focus lies mainly on local produce, meats, and dairy.

The best mezze selection will always utilize a perfect mix of local ingredients: olive oil, dairy, meat, fish, vegetables, and seasonal greens and fruit.

**Left:** Brady Black's graffiti on the streets of Beirut reveals today's intolerable political and economic tensions endured by all Lebanese.

# Hummus

## *Hummus bi Tahini*

In Lebanon, a good restaurant is measured by the quality of its hummus. The best hummus experience in Beirut is at a *fuwwel*, a food artisan shop that specializes in making just hummus, *foul* (a dish made with dried fava beans, see p. 57), and a variety of derivatives. In these establishments, hummus is often served to customers with sliced raw onion or scallions, fresh vegetables, an assortment of local pickles, and Arabic bread. The word hummus simply means *chickpeas*, but multi-colored hummus variations using a variety of ingredients are emerging locally and around the world. Adventurous chefs have mixed in beets, red pepper paste or flakes, spices, herbs, and wild greens.

In the Middle East, wars are being fought on the subject of hummus—where it originated, who makes it best, who can make the largest plate... As if we do not have enough to fight about! I tend to agree with the adage, "Make food, not war." Having said that, Lebanese hummus is the yummiest!

1½ cups (250 g) dried chickpeas

1 teaspoon baking soda (if your chickpeas are old)

1 garlic clove (optional)

½ cup (120 g) smooth, good-quality tahini (I like Cortas brand), stirred well

Juice of 1–2 lemons (add a tablespoon of bitter orange juice if you can find it)

Pinch ground cumin

Pinch cayenne or Aleppo pepper

Extra-virgin olive oil, for drizzling

Salt

In a large bowl, cover the chickpeas with plenty of water and add the baking soda, if needed. Soak overnight. The next day, rinse them under cold water, drain, and pour them into a large pot, along with fresh water to cover. Bring to a boil over high heat, then reduce the heat and simmer until the chickpeas are soft , 45 minutes to 1 hour. Test for doneness by squeezing one chickpea between your index finger and thumb; it should break apart easily. Leave to cool for 30 minutes in the cooking water. Drain the chickpeas, reserving 1 cup (240 ml) of the cooking liquid for later use.

Pour the chickpeas into a food processor or blender, setting a few aside for the garnish. Process until you have a smooth consistency. Add a pinch of salt and the garlic, if using. With the machine running, slowly pour in the tahini, followed by a little of the lemon juice. Stop the machine from time to time to taste to check if you need to add more lemon juice or salt. If the hummus is too thick, you can add some of the reserved cooking liquid until it reaches your desired texture (remember that it thickens when chilled).

Spoon the hummus into a shallow bowl or bowls. Use the back of a spoon or a wooden pestle to smooth and spread the hummus, evenly raising the edges on all sides. Sprinkle with a pinch of cumin and ground cayenne or Aleppo pepper, and drizzle with lots of olive oil. Serve with Arabic bread (p. 28).

**Variations** You can serve your hummus with a variety of delicious toppings to create a true piece of art: toasted pine nuts, cooked beef, lamb, chicken, shawarma (p. 142 and 144), *basterma* (air-dried seasoned cured beef), *sujuk* (Armenian sausages, see p. 91), or *Awarma* (Lebanese Lamb Confit, p. 197), or fresh herbs and vegetables.

# Smoky Eggplant Dip

## *Baba Ghannouj*

My first encounter with *baba ghannouj* was in my father's restaurant, Kebabs & Things, years ago in Florida. It became one of my food addictions. Every single night during my break for supper, I would make myself a plate of tabbouleh with a large spoonful of this awesome roasted eggplant dip made with tahini. Since then, I have perfected the recipe. I love the name "*ghannouj*"—in Arabic it means "to be spoiled by an excess of cuddling." That's exactly what this dish does to me, it cuddles me and makes me feel good.

2 large eggplants
¼ cup (60 g) tahini
1 lemon, freshly squeezed
1 garlic clove, crushed, or to taste
   (optional)
1 teaspoon salt, or to taste
Extra-virgin olive oil
Pinch ground cumin
Pinch Aleppo pepper or cayenne
Pomegranate seeds, to garnish
   (optional)

Use a skewer, knife, or fork to pierce holes in the skin of the eggplants. This will prevent them from bursting. Roast the eggplants (over your stovetop burner on low heat, on your grill, or under a broiler.) Turn them every so often so they cook evenly. They should be very soft to the touch with charred skin. This will take 25 to 30 minutes, depending on their size.

Cool the roasted eggplants on a plate or in a steel colander. When they are cool enough to handle, use a sharp knife to scrape the flesh from the charred skin. Remove and discard the stems. Transfer the eggplant pulp to a sieve to drain. If your eggplant has a lot of seeds, discard most of the seeds—they can be bitter and cause an unpleasant reaction in some people.

Put the pulp on a chopping board and chop with a sharp knife until you get a textured paste with no big lumps. Alternatively, carefully pulse using a handheld immersion blender—the paste should be coarse, not watery. Add the tahini, lemon juice, and crushed garlic, if using (more if you are one of those who worships the stuff), and finally salt to taste. This is where the expertise comes in. You have to taste to find a balance between the acidity of the lemon and the seasoning of the salt.

Spread the finished mixture into a serving bowl, using the back of a spoon to form a shallow well. Drizzle with lots of good quality extra-virgin olive oil, and add a sprinkle of cumin and cayenne or Aleppo pepper. Sprinkle with some pomegranate seeds to garnish, when in season.

**Variation** Finely chop 1 small onion and mix it with 1–2 tablespoons of pomegranate molasses. Use this to garnish the *baba ghanouj* to give it an extra tangy flavor.

# Rustic Whole Chickpeas

## *Balila*

*Balila* is a dish of wholesome cooked chickpeas served as nature intended—simply and unpretentiously—with a sprinkle of cumin to remind us of faraway lands. The secret lies in slow cooking the chickpeas to perfection. *Balila* is served as a mezze dish and is a favorite of customers of local *fuwwel*, traditional eateries specializing in chickpea and fava bean dishes, now mostly found in old markets in Tripoli (Lebanon's second largest city, in the north), Saida (in the south), and Tyre (one of the oldest continually inhabited cities in the world), and still a few in Beirut. Modern concepts have flourished, unfortunately threatening the traditional artisans.

1½ cups (250 g) dried chickpeas
1 teaspoon baking soda (optional)
1–2 garlic cloves, or to taste
Juice of 1–2 lemons
½ cup (120 ml) extra-virgin olive oil
2 tablespoons pine nuts
1 tablespoon clarified butter
  or butter
1 bunch flat-leaf parsley, finely
  chopped (see p. 14 for tips)
Pinch ground cumin
Pinch Aleppo pepper or cayenne
Salt

Soak the chickpeas in water with the baking soda overnight. (If the chickpeas are young, you don't need to add baking soda). The next day, rinse and drain the chickpeas, and transfer them to a pot with plenty of fresh water. Bring to a boil, then reduce the heat and simmer until the chickpeas are tender, but still hold their shape, 30 to 45 minutes depending on how fresh your dried chickpeas are. Test by squeezing a chickpea between your fingers. Leave to cool in the cooking water until lukewarm.

In a mortar and pestle, place 1 or 2 cloves of garlic, depending on how sharp the garlic is and how much you appreciate the taste. Add a pinch of salt and crush to a paste.

In a large mixing bowl, whisk the garlic, lemon juice, and olive oil until well blended.

Drain the cooked chickpeas, setting aside some of the cooking water for use later, and add the chickpeas to the bowl. Gently mix, being careful not to break the chickpeas, and season with salt to taste. If you feel that the mixture is too thick, you may add a bit of the cooking water, a tablespoon at a time.

Fry the pine nuts in the clarified butter until golden. Drain excess oil, if desired.

Garnish the chickpeas with the fried pine nuts, chopped parsley, and a pinch of cumin and cayenne or Aleppo pepper. Serve warm.

# Fava Beans in Oil

## *Foul Mudammas*

*Foul* is breakfast, the old-fashioned way—hearty and simple. This dish of slow-cooked fava beans is an ancient staple, originally from Egypt. The *fuwwel*—local eateries specializing in *foul* and hummus have kept this ancient food tradition alive. I love to visit the *fuwwel* to see the ritual unravel before me. Fava beans are simmered in large copper pots overnight, ready to serve to customers at dawn. *Foul* has also made a name for itself on our mezze table topped with bright red chopped tomatoes, parsley, lemon juice, garlic (plenty of it), and a generous drizzle of extra-virgin olive oil.

You can make this recipe the traditional way, from dried beans, or use good-quality canned beans (I use Cortas cooked fava beans). Look for them in Middle Eastern grocery stores.

1½ cups (250 g) dried fava beans,
    or two 14 oz (400 g) cans
    fava beans
1 teaspoon baking soda
    (if using dried beans)
2 garlic cloves, or to taste
Pinch of salt
Juice of 1–2 lemons
½ cup (120 ml) extra-virgin olive oil
1–2 tomatoes, finely chopped
½ bunch flat-leaf parsley,
    finely chopped
Pinch ground cumin
Pinch cayenne
1 bunch mint, leaves stripped,
    to serve
1–2 scallions, to serve
Pickles, to serve

If you are using dried fava beans: soak the fava beans overnight in plenty of water with the baking soda.

Drain the soaked or canned fava beans and rinse thoroughly under cold running water. Drain and place them in a large pot with enough fresh water to cover them. Bring to a boil, then reduce heat and simmer until the beans are very tender but still hold their shape, 1 to 1½ hours for dried beans, or 10 minutes if using canned beans. Test for doneness by squeezing a fava bean between your index finger and thumb. Drain, reserving about 1 cup (240 ml) of the cooking liquid for later use.

In a large mortar and pestle, crush the garlic to a paste with a pinch of salt. Blend in the lemon juice and olive oil and transfer to a mixing bowl. Add the drained fava beans. Mix thoroughly, crushing some of the beans using your pestle. Mix in some of the reserved cooking water, a tablespoon at a time, until your mixture is the consistency of oatmeal.

Spoon into individual serving bowls and drizzle with more olive oil for a richer flavor. Garnish the top with tomatoes and parsley and a sprinkle of cumin and cayenne. Serve warm with mint leaves, scallions, and colorful homemade pickles alongside.

SERVES 12

# Stuffed Grape Leaves in Oil

## *Warak Enab bi Zeit*

Stuffing and rolling grape leaves is a lengthy process, an acquired talent that takes practice—like many things in life. Recently, while visiting a local food fair, I purchased a device that rolls out the grape leaves automatically. Sure, it makes life easier, but as we employ modern, time-saving tools, food culture and knowledge can be lost along the way. For me, hand-rolled grape leaves are superior, and certainly more authentic. If you are lucky enough to have a grape vine growing at home, use fresh young leaves that are still tender. This is a party dish, made in a large quantity because the rolls must be tightly layered in the pot to prevent them from unrolling during cooking. Rolling leaves is a communal affair; gather some friends and family to help and enjoy the work! These are typically served as mezze, and make excellent "fridge food" for when you need a quick snack, but there is also a heartier meat version on p. 174.

70 to 80 young grape vine leaves, stems removed, or a 16 oz (450 g) jar of grape vine leaves

2 tablespoons extra-virgin olive oil

Juice of 1–2 lemons

4 potatoes, peeled and sliced into thick rounds

2 large tomatoes, sliced

1 large onion, sliced

A few lettuce leaves (optional)

Salt

**STUFFING**

1½ cups (300 g) short-grain white rice, soaked in cold water for 30 minutes

2¼ lb (1 kg) tomatoes, finely chopped

2 bunches flat-leaf parsley, finely chopped

½ bunch mint, leaves finely chopped

2 large onions, finely chopped

*Continued on next page*

If you are using fresh grape leaves, blanch them in salted boiling water for 1 minute. Immediately plunge them into ice-cold water to stop the cooking process. If using canned grape leaves, rinse thoroughly. Drain and set aside.

In a large mixing bowl, combine all of the stuffing ingredients: Start with the drained rice, then mix in the chopped vegetables, spices, and finally the lemon juice and oils. Use your hands to mix well. Taste for seasoning—You have to find the right balance between the lemon, salt and olive oil. Taste a few grains to be sure you have a tangy dressing. Put the mixture in a large sieve set over a bowl to drain. Reserve the juices for later use.

Flatten a grape leaf on the table in front of you, rough side up, with the stem end closest to you. Place 1 full teaspoon of stuffing in a horizontal line across the middle. Fold the sides inwards and roll up like a cigar. Make sure the stuffing is completely covered and the leaf is tightly and securely wrapped, but not so tight that the rice doesn't have room to expand. This is where the expertise lies. Repeat to use up all the stuffing.

Pour olive oil and lemon juice into an 8-quart (8 liter) soup pot. Place the potato, tomato, and onion slices at the bottom. Layer the stuffed grape leaves around the edge of the pot, seam side down, and then layer the rest across the middle. Add the reserved juices from the stuffing. You can cover the grape leaves with lettuce leaves to avoid oxidation. Pour in enough water to cover the top layer of leaves by about 1 in (2 cm). Place an upturned (heat-safe) plate on top of the layers in the pot to keep the grape leaves fully submerged during cooking. Cover the pot with a lid. Bring to a

1 teaspoon ground cinnamon

1 teaspoon freshly ground
  black pepper

1 teaspoon ground allspice

1 teaspoon cayenne or red pepper
  paste (p. 200, optional)

1 tablespoon salt

Juice of 1–2 lemons

¼ cup (60 ml) extra-virgin olive oil

¼ cup (60 ml) vegetable oil

boil, then reduce the heat and simmer gently for 60 to 90 minutes, until the rolls are tender and the rice is cooked. Turn off the heat, remove the lid, upturned plate, and lettuce leaves, and leave to cool to room temperature in the pot.

To serve, place a large deep serving dish face down on top of the pot. Holding the dish in place. flip the pot over onto the dish, letting the contents of the pot drop onto the serving dish. Serve at room temperature. Keeps well in the fridge for several days.

# Eggplants with Chickpeas and Tomatoes

## *Batijen Msa'ka'*

In this dish, eggplants are cooked in a rustic tomato sauce flavored with tangy pomegranate syrup. As its name suggests (*msa'ka'* means cooled), it is served at room temperature, usually with bread to scoop up the delicious sauce. You can cook it on the stovetop or finish in the oven for a rich flavor. Use in-season eggplants for best results.

¾ cup (150 g) dried chickpeas, or a
    15 oz (400 g) can chickpeas
½ teaspoon baking soda (optional)
2¼ lb (1 kg) medium eggplants
Salt and freshly ground
    black pepper
Vegetable oil, for frying
2 tablespoons extra-virgin olive oil
2 medium onions, sliced into
    half-moons
1 whole garlic bulb, peeled and
    left whole or chopped (to
    your taste)
4 tomatoes, peeled and
    finely chopped; plus 2 sliced,
    if oven-baking
2 tablespoons tomato paste diluted
    with ½ cup (120 ml) water
½ teaspoon ground cinnamon
1 tablespoon pomegranate
    molasses
Pinch ground dried mint, or
    1 tablespoon chopped fresh mint,
    to serve

Soak the dried chickpeas overnight in plenty of water. Add the baking soda to the soaking water if your dried chickpeas have been sitting in your pantry for a while. The next day, thoroughly rinse the chickpeas under cold running water, drain, and place them in a large pot with fresh water to cover them. Bring to a boil, then reduce the heat and simmer gently until tender but still holding their shape, 30 to 45 minutes. If using canned chickpeas, rinse well. Drain and set aside.

Rinse and dry the eggplants. Cut off and discard the ends. Peel vertically in stripes, then quarter them lengthwise. Arrange in a colander, sprinkle with salt, and leave to sweat for about 30 minutes to drain excess moisture. Rinse with cold water and pat dry with a kitchen towel.

Pour vegetable oil into a large pot or deep-fryer to a depth of 2 in (5 cm). Heat until the oil reaches a temperature of 350°F (180°C), or until small bubbles gather around a small piece of bread dropped into the oil. Working in batches, fry the eggplant pieces for 2 minutes, until cooked and golden. Transfer to a metal colander or a plate lined with paper towels to drain excess oil. Set aside.

Heat the olive oil in a large frying pan and sauté the onion until golden. Add the garlic and cook for 1 minute. Add the chopped tomatoes, diluted tomato paste, cinnamon, and pomegranate molasses and simmer for 10 minutes until the tomatoes soften. Add the drained chickpeas and salt and pepper to taste. Simmer for 15 minutes until the mixture thickens. You can finish the dish on the stovetop: Add the eggplants to the pan and simmer, covered, for 15 more minutes, then spoon the eggplants onto a serving dish and top with the sauce. Alternatively, finish in the oven: Preheat the oven to 400°F (200°C). Carefully arrange the eggplants in one layer in a baking dish or pan. Cover with the tomato sauce and arrange the sliced tomatoes on top. Bake for 20 minutes, until the tomatoes soften and begin to brown.

Let cool to room temperature. Sprinkle with mint just before serving.

# Spicy Potatoes

## *Batata Harra*

This recipe started my passion for red pepper paste—I absolutely insist on making it every year. It is an essential pantry item (*mouneh*) for the soul, and I splash it everywhere. It brightens the flavor of everything and wakes up the senses. Mix red pepper paste with garlic and cilantro and you've reached heaven on earth. These fiery herbed potatoes will definitely demand attention on your table, and they'll get it—trust me! Be sure to ask your grocer which variety of potato is best for frying.

2¼ lb (1 kg) starchy potatoes

Vegetable oil, for frying

2 tablespoons tomato paste diluted with ½ cup (120 ml) water

1–2 tablespoons red pepper paste (p. 200)

Juice of 2 lemons

2 cups (480 ml) chicken or vegetable stock

Salt and freshly ground black pepper

2 tablespoons extra-virgin olive oil

10 garlic cloves, crushed

1 bunch cilantro, leaves finely chopped

Peel the potatoes and cut them into cubes: Bite-size is perfect. Don't cut the potatoes too small or too big. Soak the cut potatoes in cool water as you work. Just before frying, pat them dry with a kitchen towel.

Pour vegetable oil into a large pot or deep-fryer to a depth of 2 in (5 cm). Heat until the oil reaches a temperature of 350°F (180°C), or until small bubbles gather around a small piece of potato dropped into the oil. Fry the potatoes in batches, for 3 to 5 minutes, until evenly golden. Using a slotted spoon, transfer them to a steel colander or a bowl lined with paper towels to drain excess oil. Set aside.

In a mixing bowl, combine the diluted tomato paste, red pepper paste, and lemon juice. Whisk in the stock and season to your liking with salt and pepper. Mix thoroughly.

Heat the olive oil in a large deep sauté pan, and briefly sauté the garlic. Pour in the red pepper paste mixture and simmer for about 5 minutes, until most of the liquid has evaporated and you have a creamy sauce consistency. Add the chopped cilantro and cook for an additional 2–3 minutes. This is my favorite part, when my whole house smells like cilantro and garlic! Gently stir the potatoes into the simmering sauce. Serve immediately so the potatoes remain crisp and crunchy.

# Chickpeas with Yogurt

## *Fattet Hummus*

Hummus is the word in Arabic used for both chickpeas and the dip made from them—*hummus bi tahini* (see p. 52). The Arabic word *fatteh* means to crumble. This must refer to the bread used to top this layered dish. Many versions of *fatteh* exist, replacing the chickpeas with chicken, lamb *kafta* (p. 136), fried eggplants stuffed with meat, lamb feet and tongue (believe it or not), and stuffed intestines (ooh!). The Lebanese don't waste a single piece of a butchered animal.

1½ cups (250 g) dried chickpeas

½ teaspoon baking soda (optional)

2 tablespoons pine nuts

1 tablespoon clarified butter
   or butter

1 garlic clove

1 cup (250 g) plain yogurt

1 cup (280 g) Labneh (Thick
   Strained Yogurt, p. 94) or thick
   Greek-style yogurt

2 cups bite-size squares of Arabic
   bread (p. 28), fried or toasted

Pinch ground cumin

Pinch Aleppo pepper or cayenne,
   to garnish

Salt

In a large bowl, cover the chickpeas in plenty of water and add the baking soda (if the dried chickpeas are very fresh, you may not need to add baking soda). Soak the chickpeas overnight. The next day, rinse them thoroughly under cold water, drain, and pour them into a large pot, along with fresh water to cover them. Bring to a boil over high heat, then reduce the heat and simmer until the chickpeas are tender but still hold their shape, 30 to 45 minutes. Drain the chickpeas, reserving 1 cup (240 ml) of the cooking liquid for later use.

Fry the pine nuts in the clarified butter, drain on a plate lined with paper towels, and set aside.

Crush the garlic with a bit of salt using a mortar and pestle. Combine the yogurt and labneh in a saucepan and whisk to combine. Add garlic and more salt, if needed. Heat through over very low heat, without letting the mixture boil. Don't leave it for a second; you don't want the yogurt to curdle.

Pour the hot chickpeas into a serving dish. Add cooking water, a tablespoon at a time, until they are saucy. Top with the warm yogurt mixture. Garnish with the bread and pine nuts. Sprinkle with cumin and Aleppo pepper or cayenne. Serve immediately.

# Fish Fillets with Tahini Sauce and Pine Nuts

## *Tajen*

Not to be confused with the Moroccan stew named for the pot in which it is cooked, *tajen* is a dish of baked white fish served with a lemony tahini sauce and fried pine nuts. The taste of *tajen* will take you away to the Mediterranean coast where you sit barefoot with friends, sipping arak and *mezmezzing*—a slang verb derived from the word mezze. What a dream to sit and chat and eat mezze next to the sea!

When I make *tajen* I have to keep myself from eating the fish as it comes out of the oven. If you can, make the sauce using bitter (Seville) orange juice. It will definitely make a statement.

2¼ lb (1 kg) white fish fillets, such as cod, haddock, or sea bass
½ cup (120 ml) extra-virgin olive oil
1–2 lemons, sliced
Juice of 1–2 lemons
½ cup (120 ml) vegetable oil
4 medium onions, sliced
2 garlic cloves, minced
1 green chile pepper, finely chopped (optional)
2–3 tablespoons pine nuts
1 tablespoon clarified butter or olive oil
½ bunch flat-leaf parsley, finely chopped, to serve
Salt

**TAHINI SAUCE (*TARATOR*)**
1 garlic clove
1 cup (240 ml) tahini
½ cup (120 ml) freshly squeezed lemon juice, or ¼ cup (60 ml) bitter orange juice
¾ cup (180 ml) water

Rinse and pat dry the fish, then season all over with salt. Leave it to rest in the refrigerator for 30 minutes. Preheat the oven to 425°F (220°C).

Generously brush a large piece of aluminum foil with half of the olive oil, and place the fish in the center. Arrange the lemon slices evenly across the fish and drizzle the top with the lemon juice and the rest of the olive oil. Wrap the foil securely around the fish and place on a baking pan. Bake for 15 to 20 minutes, depending on the thickness, until the fish is easily flaked with a fork. Open the foil and set aside to cool.

Meanwhile, make the *tarator*. Crush the garlic with a pinch of salt in a mortar and pestle. In a mixing bowl, blend the tahini with the lemon or bitter orange juice and water—you may wish to use a handheld immersion blender, if you have one. Mix in the crushed garlic and season to taste with salt.

Heat the vegetable oil in a large frying pan and sauté the onions until golden brown, almost caramelized. When the onions are soft, add garlic and chile, if using. Pour in the *tarator* and simmer for a minute or so. Set aside to cool.

In a small nonstick frying pan, fry the pine nuts in the clarified butter until golden brown, watching carefully since they can burn quickly. Using a slotted spoon, transfer the nuts to a plate lined with paper towels and set aside to cool.

Cut the fish into serving-sized pieces and arrange in a serving dish. Pour the sauce over the fish and sprinkle with the fried pine nuts and chopped parsley. Serve at room temperature with Arabic bread.

SERVES 4

# Chicken Livers with Pomegranate Molasses

*Asbet Djej wa Dibs Rumman*

In most Lebanese restaurants serving mezze, cooked chicken liver is served in traditional clay pots that keep the food warm until it is gobbled up. The liver is marinated in the cooking juices and pieces of Arabic bread are dipped into the juice to soak up every drop. While working in a Lebanese restaurant, a big challenge I imposed on myself (I love culinary challenges) was to thoroughly clean all the pieces of liver for the day's prep. You can imagine how fun that must have been!

1 lb (450 g) chicken livers

1 garlic clove

2 tablespoons pomegranate
  molasses

Juice of 1–2 lemons

2 tablespoons vegetable oil

Salt and freshly ground
  black pepper

A handful of cilantro or parsley
  leaves, finely chopped

It is important to clean the livers carefully, removing loose nerves or blood clots. You can ask your butcher to do this for you.

Crush the garlic with a little salt using a mortar and pestle. Add the pomegranate molasses and lemon juice, mix well, and set aside.

In a frying pan, sauté the chicken livers in the oil, until lightly golden, just slightly pink in the center (but never bloody or raw), and they reach an internal temperature of 160°F (70°C). Don't overcook them or the pieces will become rubbery. Add the crushed garlic mixture and mix well. Season with salt and pepper to taste. Garnish with the chopped cilantro or parsley and serve warm.

# Falafel

Falafel is Lebanese street food *par excellence*, but can also be found on a mezze table. Every Thursday, after my children attended their theater class, it was falafel night at the Massaad home. We would order falafel from Sahyoun, one of the oldest and most famous falafel shops in Lebanon. Customers arrive from the poorest neighborhoods and the wealthiest to eat falafel sandwiches here. If it was my turn to pick up the children, I always arrived a bit early to hang out with the owner, Mr. Zouheir, and talk about philosophy and life. The smell of cooking falafel reminds me of when I use to make daily batches in our family restaurant in Florida. I still use the same falafel mold at home today that I worked with almost 35 years ago. I am very attached to it.

There are many variations of this recipe. Some make falafel using only fava beans, others just chickpeas, while others mix the two. Traditional Lebanese falafel shops don't add parsley or cilantro, though in neighboring countries it's commonly done. This is my version. Don't be afraid of the quantity—they go quickly.

1½ cups (250 g) dried fava beans

1½ cups (250 g) dried chickpeas

1 teaspoon baking soda

1 large onion, quartered

7–8 garlic cloves, peeled

1 chile pepper (optional)

2 teaspoons ground coriander

1 tablespoon ground cumin

½ teaspoon ground black pepper

½ teaspoon ground allspice

Pinch ground cinnamon

1 teaspoon salt, or to taste

½ teaspoon cayenne (optional)

Pinch ground cardamom

Pinch nutmeg, freshly ground

1 tablespoon baking powder

½ cup (70 g) sesame seeds (optional)

Vegetable oil, for frying

**TO SERVE (OPTIONAL)**

Arabic bread (p. 28)

Tahini sauce (*tarator*, p. 68)

Sliced tomatoes, fresh herbs, and/or
    pickled chiles or turnips (p. 203)

Soak the fava beans and chickpeas for 24 hours in cold water in separate bowls, each with ½ teaspoon of baking soda. Rinse thoroughly and drain. In a food processor, grind the fava beans, chickpeas, onion, garlic, chile peppers (if using), and seasonings together to a coarse paste. If the batter is too thick, thin the mixture with a tablespoon of water at a time. Refrigerate for at least 1 hour, or overnight for better results. About 10 minutes before shaping and frying, mix in the baking powder. Knead well and leave to rest for 10 minutes.

Pour vegetable oil into a large pot or deep-fryer to a depth of 2 in (5 cm). Heat until the oil reaches a temperature of 350°F (180°C), or until small bubbles gather around a small piece of falafel mixture dropped into the oil.

You can shape the falafel mixture into patties about 1 in (2.5 cm) in diameter using moistened hands. Or, if you have a falafel mold, first dip it in water, then use it to scoop falafel mixture and form the patties. For best results don't flatten the top of the mixture in the mold, shape it into a pyramid using a pastry knife. Dip the falafel into the sesame seeds, if using, then carefully drop it into the hot oil. Deep-fry the falafel in small batches for 3–4 minutes until golden brown on both sides. They will start to float when they are ready. Using a slotted spoon, transfer to a colander to drain excess oil.

Serve as a mezze with *tarator* on the side, or in sandwiches with Arabic bread, sliced tomatoes, fresh mint leaves, coarsely chopped parsley, and pickled green chile peppers and/or turnips, and a generous drizzle of *tarator* on top.

# Lebanese Sausages

## *Maqaneq*

Sausages made of rich ground meat (beef, lamb, or both) seasoned with ground spices (cinnamon, cumin, cloves, coriander, nutmeg, and black and white pepper) really hits the spot when it's produced by a qualified food artisan. If I were to make *maqaneq* from scratch, I would add a pinch of fennel seeds—Italian cuisine has always inspired me. The sausages are full of flavor, all one needs to cook them is a bit of lemon juice and/or pomegranate molasses to make this scrumptious bite simply amazing! I've seen guests lick their fingers not to waste a single drop. I have a friend who splashes in a spoonful of arak (a Levantine anise spirit) to flambé the sausages just before serving. This creates a burst of flames which makes the alcohol in the arak evaporate, resulting in a fairly thick caramelized sauce with more aroma and flavor.

1 lb (450 g) Lebanese beef or lamb sausages (*maqaneq*), North African *merguez* sausages, or any good-quality sausages
1 tablespoon vegetable oil
2 tablespoons pomegranate molasses (I like Cortas brand)
1 tablespoon arak (optional)

If your sausages are long, separate them into smaller sausages: Using your index finger and thumb, press firmly into a sausage at 1½ to 2 in (4 to 5 cm) intervals to separate the meat within, and then twist the sausage casing to secure. Using kitchen scissors, cut at the twist to separate. Repeat with remaining sausages.

Fry sausages in oil in a frying pan, turning them occasionally, until just cooked through, 8 to 10 minutes. They must stay juicy inside and firm on the outside; If you overcook them they become rubbery. Pour off all but about a tablespoon of the rendered fat in the pan. Add the pomegranate molasses to deglaze the pan, stirring well. If using, pour in the arak and carefully ignite the liquid until the alcohol burns off. Transfer the sausages to a serving dish and pour the juices on top. Serve immediately.

# Fried Vegetables

## *Khodra Mekliyeh*

This is a simple dish, but adds just the right note to a mezze selection. I use whatever vegetables are seasonally available, but my absolute favorite is eggplant. You can easily adjust the quantities according to the size of your crowd. Use the dressing below, or serve them with *tarator* (tahini sauce, p. 68).

2 medium eggplants

2½ lb (1 kg) cauliflower, cut into 2-inch (5 cm) florets

4 small zucchini, sliced lengthwise about ¼ in (6 mm) thick

Vegetable oil, for frying

Salt

**DRESSING (OPTIONAL)**

1 garlic clove

2 tablespoons pomegranate molasses

½ cup (120 ml) extra-virgin olive oil

Start with the eggplants because they take more time to prepare. Rinse them and dry with a clean kitchen towel. Cut off and discard the ends, then peel the skin in lengthwise stripes. Cut horizontally into evenly sized rounds about ½ in (1 cm) thick. Arrange the slices in a colander, sprinkle with salt, and leave to sweat for about 30 minutes. Rinse with cold water. Pat each one with a dry kitchen towel and set aside.

Rinse and dry the cauliflower and set them aside on a separate plate. Rinse and dry the zucchini. Cut off and discard the ends, and slice them horizontally into ½ in (1 cm) rounds and set aside on another plate.

Pour vegetable oil into a large pot or deep-fryer to a depth of 2 in (5 cm). Heat until the oil reaches a temperature of 350°F (180°C), or until small bubbles gather around a small piece of bread dropped into the oil. Working in batches, fry the vegetables (without mixing them) in the oil for 3–4 minutes, until golden brown. They will start to float when they are ready. Using a slotted spoon, transfer them to a colander to drain excess oil.

Meanwhile, make the dressing, if using: Crush the garlic with a pinch of salt in a mortar and pestle. Mix in the pomegranate molasses and extra-virgin olive oil. Season with salt to taste.

Arrange the fried vegetables on a plate, sprinkle with a pinch of salt, and serve immediately with a drizzle of dressing.

# Wild Chicory in Oil

## *Hindbeh bi Zeit*

This is a popular vegetarian dish that is often served as part of a lavish mezze. The slightly bitter flavor of chicory is wonderful, but any type of wild edible greens or cooking greens from your farmers' market will work perfectly.

2¼ lb (1 kg) wild chicory, dandelion greens, or other bitter greens
½ cup (120 ml) extra-virgin olive oil
4 onions, sliced
Salt and freshly ground black pepper
Lemon wedges, to serve

Trim the chicory stems, wash the leaves, and coarsely chop them. Blanch leaves in salted boiling water for 1 minute. Immediately transfer them to cold water to stop the cooking process. Drain and squeeze out excess water with your hands.

Heat 2 tablespoons of the olive oil in a large frying pan and sauté the onions until golden brown and caramelized. Transfer half of the onions to a plate, leaving the rest in the pan.

Add the chicory leaves to the pan with the remaining 6 tablespoons of oil. Cook, stirring, for a few minutes to heat through. Sprinkle salt and pepper to taste. Arrange on a serving plate and top with the reserved onions and lemon wedges. Serve at room temperature.

# Minced Lamb Tartare

*Habra Nayeh*

A meal involving a vast mezze spread is a central part of celebrations across Lebanon. Traditionally, this warrants the slaying of an animal—usually a goat or sheep (the type of meat used often depends on the region). Today, this is a ritual practiced mostly in mountain villages around the country, where animals are raised for their milk and eventually their meat. Not only is a raw meat platter essential to a celebratory mezze spread, for some people it's the very best part. The meat must be exceptionally fresh for this dish—the butcher is often a trusted family friend or a relative. Today, this type of traditional festive platter, which also often includes raw kibbeh, see pp. 111 and 112, is also available in restaurants serving mezze as their specialty. Each recipe is very special.

This recipe can be easily doubled for a celebration, but leftovers should not be eaten raw (they can be cooked). A few words of warning: Raw meat consumption is not recommended for pregnant women. Choose a reliable source for your meat. If at all possible (and that's just me living in an ideal world), buy very fresh humanely-raised, organic meat to minimize any risk.

10½ oz (300 g) lamb tenderloin
   (or use goat or beef tenderloin)
½ teaspoon salt, or to taste

**TO SERVE**
1 bunch mint, leaves stripped
1 small onion, sliced
2–4 green chile peppers (optional)
Garlic sauce (*toum*, p. 130)
Arabic bread (p. 28)

When grinding meat for raw consumption, put the meat in the freezer 30 minutes before processing for better results. Whether you use the traditional stone mortar and wooden pestle (*jorn*, see p. 105) or a food processor, the same rule applies. Should it be impossible for you to freeze the meat in advance, you can add 2 ice cubes as you work.

Put the meat into the food processor, add the salt, and begin processing at a low speed. Gradually increase the speed until the meat has a cream-like consistency. If you are using a mortar and pestle, pound the meat hard, using a spatula to clean the sides of the mortar from time to time. It takes muscles and practice to grind the meat in a mortar but it is lots of fun. Lebanese people believe that the taste is quite different and more authentic when made like this.

Arrange on a platter and serve with fresh mint leaves, raw onion, green chile peppers, garlic sauce, and Arabic bread.

# Fried Whitebait

## *Samak Bizri*

This is a favorite dish for us Lebanese. We simply love our *samak bizri*. These tiny fish, deep-fried and eaten whole, are occasionally cooked at home during their season, but they are more typically enjoyed with a cold drink in coastal restaurants overlooking the Mediterranean Sea. The fish do not need to be drenched in flour—just a sprinkle will prevent them from sticking together during frying.

1 lb (450 g) tiny whole fish (whitebait), fresh sardines, or blue anchovies, about 2 in (5 cm) long
½ cup (60 g) all-purpose flour
1 tablespoon ground sumac
Vegetable oil, for deep-frying
Tahini sauce (*tarator*, p. 68), to serve
Lemon wedges, to serve
Salt

Pick through the fish and discard any damaged ones. Place in a colander, rinse, and drain well. Generously season the fish with salt while they are still in the colander.

In a large, shallow dish, mix the flour and sumac. Working in batches, lightly dust the fish with the flour mixture, tossing them in the air to coat them evenly.

Pour vegetable oil into a large pot or deep-fryer to a depth of 2 in (5 cm). Heat until the oil reaches a temperature of 350°F (180°C), or until small bubbles gather around a small piece of bread dropped into the oil. Working in batches, fry the fish for 3–4 minutes, stirring them around, until golden brown and crisp. Using a slotted spoon, shake off excess oil and drain on a plate or steel colander lined with paper towels.

Serve hot with tahini sauce and lemon wedges.

# Frog Legs

## *Dafaade'*

When I was a young girl of seven or eight, my father had a friend with a long beard called Gilbert. He was the son of Pepe Abed, a legendary restaurateur from Byblos. Once in a while he would show up at our house to cook scrumptious, succulent frog legs in my mother's kitchen. I would lick my fingers clean (I was a child with no manners then). To this day, I cannot forget the amazing taste!

12 frog legs
1 teaspoon salt, plus a pinch
¼ teaspoon ground white pepper, plus a pinch
1 cup (120 g) all-purpose flour
Vegetable oil, for deep-frying
2 tablespoons clarified butter or butter
3–4 garlic cloves, crushed
Juice of 2–3 lemons
1 bunch cilantro, leaves finely chopped
Lemon wedges, to serve

Wash the frog legs well with cold water. Drain and leave to dry or pat dry with paper towels. Season on all sides with the salt and pepper. Spread the flour on a plate and, working in batches, coat the frog legs evenly with flour, shaking off excess. Transfer to another plate and set aside.

Pour vegetable oil into a large pot or deep-fryer to a depth of 2 in (5 cm). Heat until the oil reaches a temperature of 350°F (180°C), or until small bubbles gather around a small piece of bread dropped into the oil. Working in batches, fry the frog legs for 4–5 minutes, without letting them brown. Using a slotted spoon, shake off excess oil and drain on a plate or steel colander lined with paper towels. Set aside.

Melt the clarified butter in a large frying pan over medium heat, add the garlic, and sauté for 1 minute. Add the frog legs, sprinkle with a pinch of salt and pepper, and sauté for another minute. Add the lemon juice and briefly toss. Add the cilantro and toss again. Remove from the heat and serve the frog legs hot, with lemon wedges on the side.

# Chicken Wings with Cilantro and Garlic

## *Jawaneh Djej ma' Kozbara wa Toum*

The flavors of garlic and cilantro, intensified by the lemon juice, give these chicken wings their unforgettable flavor. For most Lebanese, this dish will stir up childhood memories. But regardless of where your guests are from, don't be surprised to see them licking their fingers! This recipe can easily be doubled if you are cooking for a crowd.

8 chicken wings

1 cup (120 g) all-purpose flour

2 garlic cloves

4 tablespoons clarified butter
  or butter

Juice of 1–2 lemons

1 bunch cilantro, leaves finely
  chopped

1 cup (240 ml) chicken stock
  (homemade is best)

Salt

Generously season the chicken wings with salt. Spread the flour on a plate and dip the wings into the flour to coat them evenly on all sides. Set aside.

Using a mortar and pestle, crush the garlic with a little salt. Heat the clarified butter in a large frying pan over medium heat and fry the crushed garlic until fragrant. Add the chicken wings and cook, turning them from time to time, until golden brown and cooked through, 10 to 15 minutes. Add the lemon juice, cilantro, and chicken stock. Cook for an additional 1–2 minutes until the liquid evaporates, then add more salt to taste, if needed. Serve hot.

# Eggs with Lamb Confit

*Bayd wa Awarma*

*Awarma*—ground lamb preserved in its own fat—is a prized ingredient, traditionally made in the villages of Lebanon to store meat without refrigeration. Nowadays, it is used for its rich flavor. This is a favorite way to eat it, with eggs cooked in a *fekhar*—a traditional pottery cooking pan. Serve it as mezze, or as a decadent breakfast.

2 large eggs, at room temperature

3 tablespoons *Awarma* (Lebanese Lamb Confit, p. 197)

¼ teaspoon ground allspice (optional)

Salt

Carefully crack the eggs into a mixing bowl without breaking the yolks. Heat a *fekhar* or frying pan over low heat. Add the *awarma* and cook until it melts. Raise the heat to medium and gently pour the eggs over the cooked *awarma*. Sprinkle with the allspice and salt, to taste. Cook until the whites are firm and the yolk has thickened, but still gooey in the middle (or to your desired doneness). Serve immediately.

# Armenian Sausages with Tomatoes

## *Sujuk wa Banadoura*

As I write this recipe, a sudden craving sets in. Thanks to the Armenian community in Lebanon, *sujuk* has become popular in street-corner bakeries, snack shops, restaurants, and Lebanese households all around the country. The sausages are made of ground beef with plenty of fat (that's what makes them so sinfully delicious), and a mixture of spices and aromatics, including allspice, cumin, chile powder, coriander, salt, and lots of garlic. The mixture is carefully stuffed into casings and air-dried under the watchful eye of the butcher or the daring home cook who takes on the task. Add a couple of fresh eggs to the *sujuk* and cooked tomatoes—see what happens!

1 lb (450 g) Armenian sausage (*sujuk*), or use merguez or spicy Italian sausages

1 tablespoon vegetable oil

4 tomatoes, peeled and coarsely chopped

Juice of 1 lemon (optional)

Cut the sausages into ¼ in (6 mm) slices. Fry in a large frying pan with oil, until browned and cooked through, 1 to 2 minutes per side. Pour off the excess fat. Add the tomatoes and cook until they begin to break down, about 5 minutes. Add the lemon juice, if using. Serve warm.

# Spiced Cheese with Tomatoes, Peppers, and Onions

## *Shankleesh*

*Shankleesh* is a dried and aged cheese made with cow, sheep, or goat milk and often flavored with spices or herbs. It is fermented for up to a month before consumption or eaten young and fresh, depending on your preference. You can find *shankleesh* vacuum-packed or preserved in oil in well-stocked Middle Eastern grocery stores, or you can substitute aged feta with a pinch of *za'atar* (see p. 31) or ground red pepper. (If you would like to try your hand at making your own *shankleesh*, you can find a recipe in my book *Mouneh: Preserving for the Lebanese Pantry*.)

7 oz (200 g) *shankleesh* or
   aged feta cheese
1 teaspoon *za'atar* (optional)
Pinch ground cayenne or
   Aleppo pepper (optional)
1 medium onion, finely chopped
1–2 tomatoes, finely chopped
1 bell pepper, finely chopped
Extra-virgin olive oil
Handful of fresh herb sprigs,
   to garnish (optional)

Crumble the cheese onto a shallow serving plate and sprinkle with *za'atar* and ground cayenne or Aleppo pepper, if using. Add the chopped onion, tomatoes, and bell pepper. When it's time to eat, simply mix all the ingredients together, drizzle with olive oil, and garnish with fresh herbs. Serve with warm Arabic bread (p. 28).

# Thick Strained Yogurt

## *Labneh*

We Lebanese are born with an *aarous labneh* (strained yogurt sandwich) in our hands. Labneh is our comfort food, an everyday staple, and one of the most precious and delicious foods we eat. Eating labneh is an occasion to bake fresh bread at home, to celebrate. It can be served simply with a drizzle of oil and Arabic bread for breakfast or a snack, or flavored with garlic as in the recipe below. It makes a wonderful accompaniment to *Man'oushé bi Za'atar* (Wild Thyme Flatbread, p. 31), and it is preserved in oil to make the Lebanese pantry staple, *Labneh Mouka'zaleh bi Zeit* (p. 198).

4 cups (900 g) plain yogurt,
 preferably full-fat (see p. 196
 to make your own)
1¾ tablespoons salt

Line a large bowl with a double layer of sterilized cheesecloth, leaving plenty of cloth overhanging the sides. Spoon the yogurt into the cheesecloth in the bowl, add the salt, and mix thoroughly. Tie the ends of the cloth together over the yogurt and secure with a string. Suspend the parcel over your sink (as is tradition) or over a bowl placed in the refrigerator, and leave to drain for up to 2 days, until the contents are firm. To test for firmness, the yogurt should easily come away from the cheesecloth.

# Thick Strained Yogurt with Garlic

## *Labneh wa Toum*

A typical mezze dish consists of labneh made with cow's milk, seasoned with garlic and fresh or dried mint leaves.

2 cups (450 g) Labneh
 (Thick Strained Yogurt)
1 garlic clove, crushed
Extra-virgin olive oil, for drizzling
Handful fresh mint leaves, or a
 pinch ground dried mint

In a mixing bowl, combine the labneh and garlic in a bowl. Blend thoroughly using a whisk. Transfer the labneh to a shallow serving bowl and spread with the back of a spoon to form a shallow well. Drizzle generously with good extra-virgin olive oil and sprinkle with fresh mint leaves or a pinch of dried mint. Serve with Arabic bread (p. 28).

# Shrimp with Garlic and Cilantro

*Kraydes ma' Kozbara wa Toum*

Your kitchen will have a delightful aroma when you cook this shrimp dish with cilantro, garlic, and butter. This is a simple and quick mezze with so much flavor. You can cook calamari in the same way (see p. 98), but I suggest grilling the rings before tossing them in the sauce (a little trick I learned from the Italians).

1 lb (450 g) extra-large peeled raw shrimp (fresh or frozen)

3–4 garlic cloves

2 tablespoons clarified butter or butter

Salt and freshly ground black pepper

Juice of 1 lemon

Pinch Aleppo pepper or cayenne

1 bunch cilantro, leaves finely chopped (reserve a few sprigs to serve)

Lemon wedges, to serve

If using frozen shrimp, place them in a colander and rinse them under cold running water to thaw, then shake to drain well.

Using a mortar and pestle, crush the garlic with pinch of salt. Melt the clarified butter in a large frying pan over medium heat. Add the crushed garlic and sauté for 1 minute. Add the shrimp, sprinkle with salt and pepper, and cook for 2–3 minutes, just until opaque. Add the lemon juice and stir gently to thoroughly coat the shrimp. Add the Aleppo pepper or cayenne, toss, add the cilantro, and gently toss again. Garnish with cilantro sprigs and lemon wedges and serve immediately.

# Fried Calamari

## *Calamari Mekliyeh*

Squid rings are typically prepared in two different ways for mezze. We either cook them with garlic, lemon, and cilantro, as we do with shrimp (p. 97), or we batter and deep-fry them and serve them with *tarator* (tahini sauce, p. 68). Fried calamari will disappear in seconds, especially if there are children around.

1 lb (450 g) cleaned squid, bodies
   sliced into ¼ in (6 mm) thick rings,
   or 1 lb (450 g) frozen calamari
   rings, thawed
1 cup (150 g) coarse semolina
Vegetable oil, for deep-frying
Salt and ground white pepper
Tahini sauce (*tarator*, p. 68),
   to serve
Lemon wedges, to serve

Generously season the squid with salt and pepper. Spread the semolina on a plate and, working in batches, coat the rings with semolina, shaking off the excess. Transfer to another plate.

Pour vegetable oil into a large pot or deep-fryer to a depth of 2 in (5 cm). Heat until the oil reaches a temperature of 350°F (180°C), or until small bubbles gather around a small piece of squid dropped into the oil. Working in batches, fry the rings just until very pale golden, about 2 minutes, being careful not to overcook them. Using a slotted spoon, shake off excess oil and transfer to a plate or steel colander lined with paper towels to drain. Set aside.

Serve hot, with *tarator* and lemon wedges on the side.

# Snails

## *Bezzek*

Snails are a very special seasonal addition to our mezze table. At the first sign of winter rains, vendors line the streets of Dora, a suburb of Beirut, to sell fresh snails that have been harvested at night by lamplight in rural regions of Lebanon. Unbelievable quantities will be showcased on the back of a pickup truck and customers will pull over to buy them. Our traditional recipe is not too fancy, but I assure you it is delicious.

24 snails, cleaned (canned ok)

1 teaspoon coarse sea salt

1 small cinnamon stick

1 bay leaf

½ onion, peeled and left intact

1–2 fresh lemon leaves

½ lemon, cut into wedges

1 small bunch fresh sumac berries, if you can find them (optional)

1–2 cups (240–480 ml) tahini sauce (*tarator*, p. 68)

Place the snails in a pot and fill with cold water. Bring to a boil, skimming any foam that rises to the surface. Add the salt, cinnamon stick, bay leaf, onion, lemon leaves, lemon wedges, and sumac. The sumac and lemon will help prevent the buildup of scum. Pre-cooked canned snails only need 5 minutes; small fresh snails need to cook for 30 to 40 minutes, and larger snails may take up to 1 hour. Test for doneness by using a toothpick to remove the snail from its cavity: If it comes out easily, then the snail is done.

Drain the snails, let them cool enough to handle, remove from their shells, and mix with the tahini sauce. Serve at room temperature.

KIBBEH

# KIBBEH

Kibbeh is considered one of our most cherished national dishes. It is made of seasoned ground lamb, beef, or mashed vegetables kneaded together with bulgur, and served raw, fried, baked, grilled on charcoal, or simmered in a sauce. It comes in all shapes and forms—there are vegetarian varieties popular with those who don't eat meat, including kibbeh made with pumpkin, potatoes, lentils (an Armenian specialty), tomatoes (a Southern specialty), chickpeas, and recently red beets. Kibbeh is eaten as part of the mezze or cooked in various sauces for a hearty main dish, served with rice. Kibbeh is produced and cooked differently across the country. From the north to the south of Lebanon, there is a whole range of regional varieties. Its diversity is derived from local traditions and regionally available ingredients.

In Beirut, *Kibbeh bi Saniyeh* (Baked Kibbeh, p. 116), is very popular and often part of the weekly family repertoire. It is made with finely ground lamb or beef, mixed with bulgur, onion, and spices and pressed into a baking pan. The dish consists of two layers of this mixture, with a ground meat stuffing (*hashwi*) in between. The stuffing is made of cooked ground meat with chopped onion and roasted pine nuts. The "meat cake" is then scored with a sharp knife into diamond shapes with a generous drizzle of olive oil to bake. On special occasions, especially when citrus fruits are in season, kibbeh balls are cooked in a citrus tahini sauce.

In the north of Lebanon, goats herd on high mountains therefore raw kibbeh is made mostly with goat meat. In Zghorta, they pride themselves on their *Kibbeh Zghartawiyeh* or *Shimaliyee* (see p. 122), where one variety is stuffed with animal fat, garlic, and dried mint, cooked on an open fire. Fresh raw meat kibbeh is also made with tender loving care by pounding it in a huge mortar with a large pestle called a *jorn.* The *jorn* sits outside a village house. It takes a lot of strength to pound the meat, and most women who do this exercise develop muscles in their arms. In the past, children would gather around to get a glimpse of the show, hoping to get a bite. The beating of the pestle in the mortar would emit a sound throughout the village—almost like a symphony.

In the Bekaa Valley, known for its *kishk* (a fine powder made from dried fermented cracked wheat and yogurt, see p. 8), kibbeh is cooked in *kishk* soup to make a warm hearty meal. In the Chouf, a steaming bowl of kibbeh soaked in warm yogurt with *awarma*, a traditional spiced lamb confit (p. 197), is very much appreciated during winter months, making use of preserved food from the pantry (*mouneh*).

On the coast of Tripoli, where fish is abundant, kibbeh is made with finely ground fish instead of meat, mixed with bulgur, white pepper, and salt. The mixture is made into stuffed balls or layered in a round baking dish, stuffed with a mixture of nuts, greens, and chickpeas. In the South of Lebanon, raw kibbeh is pounded on a marble slab mixed with bulgur and a local mixture of spices. In Sidon, flat, saucer-shaped *kibbeh sajiyeh* are stuffed with butter mixed with walnuts and hot red pepper paste. This type of stuffing is typical in Syria.

The list of different types of kibbeh made in Lebanon is long! The recipes I have chosen will get you started.

**Right:** It is not uncommon to see women in Beirut beating their carpets on their balconies at the first sign of sunshine.

# Kibbeh Balls

## *Kibbeh Iras*

These spiced bulgur meatballs with a meat and pine nut stuffing are perfect finger food—so much good stuff all in one bite. During large gatherings, it is not uncommon to see mothers encouraging their little ones to eat kibbeh to ensure they have a nourishing meal amid all the excitement. Kibbeh balls are an important part of our mezze table and a main ingredient in several stews and baked dishes (in some dishes, they can be left unstuffed; the shell mixture is simply formed into hollow balls). To quote Maria Doueihi, a local food producer, "There is no bad kibbeh, only bad meat." Make sure you source the best quality ingredients and don't be discouraged if they don't look perfect the first time around—it takes practice. In fact, those Lebanese households who can afford some luxury hire a cook who specializes in kibbeh to come once a month to make kibbeh in all shapes to store in the freezer. We take our kibbeh very seriously! You can easily double this recipe to make a bigger batch.

1 small onion, quartered

8 oz (225 g) lean ground lamb leg
   or beef sirloin

½ teaspoon ground allspice

¼ teaspoon ground cinnamon
   (optional)

¼ teaspoon freshly ground
   black pepper

½ teaspoon salt

Ice cubes

2½ cups (400 g) fine brown bulgur

Vegetable oil, for deep-frying

*Continued on next page*

To make the kibbeh shell mixture, very finely chop the onion in a food processor. Add the ground meat, along with the spices and salt and a couple of ice cubes. Blend until you have a smooth, creamy paste. Wash and drain the bulgur well, then add it to the meat mixture. Pulse for 1 minute to combine. Transfer to a mixing bowl.

Prepare a small bowl of ice water. Dipping your hands into the ice water periodically to prevent sticking, knead the mixture for a few minutes until smooth and uniform.

To make the stuffing, melt ½ tablespoon of the clarified butter in a frying pan. Sauté the pine nuts until golden brown, watching carefully so they don't burn. Remove with a slotted spoon and set aside on paper towels to drain. Add the rest of the clarified butter to the pan and sauté the onion until translucent. Stir in the ground meat, salt, and spices and cook, breaking up the meat with a wooden spoon, until well browned, 8 to 10 minutes. Once cooked, stir in the fried pine nuts and set aside.

Again moistening your hands with the cold water, divide the shell mixture into even balls each about the size of a walnut. Place one ball in your hand. Poke a hole in the ball using the index finger of your other hand, and rotate your finger to make a hollow. The walls of the shell should be an even ½ in (1 cm) thick and the length about 3 in (8 cm). Be careful not pierce the bottom or sides of the shell. Spoon about 2 teaspoons of the stuffing into the hollow and pinch the opening together with moistened

## STUFFING

1 tablespoon clarified butter
  or butter
¼ cup (35 g) pine nuts
1 small onion, finely chopped
9 oz (250 g) coarsely ground lamb
  or beef with 20% fat
¼ teaspoon salt
¼ teaspoon ground allspice
¼ teaspoon ground cumin
  (optional)
½ tablespoon pomegranate
  molasses (optional)

fingers to seal the opening, forming the kibbeh into a football shape. Repeat with the remaining shell mixture and stuffing.

At this stage, you can freeze them (first spaced out on a tray, then in sealed containers or bags; fry them from frozen), use them in recipes calling for kibbeh balls, or proceed to frying.

Pour vegetable oil into a large pot or deep-fryer to a depth of 2 in (5 cm). Heat until the oil reaches a temperature of 350°F (180°C), or until small bubbles gather around a small piece of bread dropped into the oil. Working in batches, deep-fry the kibbeh for 3–4 minutes until golden brown on all sides. Using a slotted spoon, transfer to a colander to drain excess oil.

Serve warm or at room temperature.

# Pumpkin Kibbeh

## *Kibbet Lakteen*

Meatless kibbeh is usually prepared during Lent in Lebanon for those who abstain from eating meat for religious reasons. It is also very popular with vegetarians. The color and sweetness of pumpkin balance the stuffing of hearty greens, chickpeas, and nuts in this rustic, wholesome dish.

2¼ lb (1 kg) pumpkin or butternut squash, peeled and cut into chunks

1 cup (200 g) fine white bulgur

2 tablespoons all-purpose flour

1 medium onion, grated

1 teaspoon finely chopped fresh marjoram, or ¼ teaspoon dried

¼ teaspoon ground dried mint

Grated zest of 1 lemon

Grated zest of 1 orange

1 teaspoon salt

¼ teaspoon ground black pepper

¼ teaspoon ground cinnamon

Vegetable oil, for deep-frying

### STUFFING

2 tablespoon extra-virgin olive oil

1 medium onion, sliced

14 oz (400 g) Swiss chard, kale, sorrel, or spinach, stems and leaves separated and finely chopped

1 cup (160 g) cooked chickpeas

½ cup (50 g) shelled walnuts, toasted and coarsely chopped

1 tablespoon lemon juice

½ teaspoon ground Lebanese 7-spice (*baharat*)

1 tablespoon ground sumac

1 teaspoon salt

To make the kibbeh shell mixture: Bring a large pot of water to a boil and boil the pumpkin pieces until tender, about 30 minutes. Drain and transfer to a large bowl, squeezing out excess water. Add the dry bulgur and flour and mash and mix well. Add the onion, marjoram, mint, lemon and orange zests, salt, pepper, and cinnamon and mix well. With moistened hands, knead the mixture for a few minutes until smooth and uniform. Cover loosely with a kitchen towel and set aside for 2 hours.

Meanwhile, make the stuffing: Heat the olive oil in a large sauté pan over medium heat. Sauté the onion until soft, add the coarse stems from the greens, and continue to cook until they begin to soften. Add the greens and cook, stirring, until wilted and the excess moisture has evaporated (spinach will take a little longer than chard or kale). Remove from the heat and stir in the chickpeas, walnuts, lemon juice, and spices. Transfer to a bowl and set aside.

Again moistening your hands with cold water, divide the shell mixture into even balls each about the size of a walnut. Place one ball in your hand. Poke a hole in the ball using the index finger of your other hand, and rotate your finger to make a hollow. The walls of the shell should be an even ½ in (1 cm) thick and the length about 3 in (8 cm). Be careful not pierce the bottom or sides. Spoon about 2 teaspoons of the stuffing into the hollow and pinch the opening together to seal, forming the kibbeh into a football shape. Repeat with the remaining shell mixture and stuffing.

At this stage, you can freeze them (first spaced out on a tray, then in sealed containers or bags; fry them from frozen), or proceed to frying.

Pour vegetable oil into a large pot or deep-fryer to a depth of 2 in (5 cm). Heat until the oil reaches a temperature of 350°F (180°C), or until small bubbles gather around a small piece of bread dropped into the oil. Working in batches, deep-fry the kibbeh for 3–4 minutes until golden brown on all sides. Using a slotted spoon, transfer to a colander to drain excess oil. Serve warm or at room temperature.

# Raw Kibbeh

## *Kibbeh Nayeh*

This raw meat kibbeh dish is an essential part of a lavish traditional mezze, which typically necessitated the slaying of an animal (see p. 78). In Lebanon, the type of meat used varies regionally. In villages around Lebanon, women with strong arm muscles will still grind the meat rhythmically by hand, using a large pestle and *jorn* (a large stone mortar) as their ancestors did in the past, though a food processor speeds up this task. When the meat is silky smooth, they run a knife through it to catch any impurities such as small nerves, veins, cartilage or tendon. The pounded meat is then kneaded by hand with onions, fresh herbs, salt, pepper, and bulgur, drizzled with olive oil, and served with fresh herbs and Arabic bread. Some garnish *kibbeh nayeh* with the warm stuffing from kibbeh balls (p. 106). Or you can add a teaspoon of red pepper paste (p. 200) to this recipe for a spicy variation that is popular in Syria.

A few tips: Choose a very reliable source for your meat and make sure it is organic and very fresh. Always eat *kibbeh nayeh* on the same day it is made (leftovers can be cooked).

5½ oz (150 g) ground lamb tenderloin or ground beef sirloin
Pinch salt
Ice cubes
1 tablespoon fine brown bulgur
½ teaspoon onion, grated or very finely chopped
4 fresh mint leaves, finely chopped
½ teaspoon fresh marjoram (or basil) leaves, finely chopped

**TO SERVE**
Extra-virgin olive oil, for drizzling
Fresh mint sprigs
Scallions, trimmed
Arabic bread (p. 28)

Whether you use the traditional stone mortar and wooden pestle (*jorn*) or a food processor, the same rule applies. Put the meat in the freezer for 30 minutes before processing for best results. Should it be impossible for you to freeze the meat in advance, you can add 2 ice cubes as you work. Put the meat into the food processor, add a pinch of salt, and begin processing at a low speed. Gradually increase the speed until the meat is finely ground with a cream-like consistency. If you would like to use a mortar and pestle, pound the meat hard with the salt until you have a paste. Use a spatula to scrape down the sides of the mortar periodically. It takes muscles and practice to achieve a smooth, creamy consistency. Run a knife through it to gather any impurities.

Prepare a small bowl of ice water. Briefly rinse the bulgur and squeeze out excess water. Place it in a large mixing bowl, along with the ground meat, onion, mint, and marjoram. Moistening your hands in the ice water to prevent sticking, knead the mixture with your hands until smooth and evenly mixed.

Spread the kibbeh onto a plate and flatten to about 1 in (2 cm) thick. Make grooves in the surface with your fingers so the olive oil can seep in. Serve immediately or keep in the fridge for 30 minutes at most. Drizzle with plenty of olive oil before serving with mint leaves and scallions.

# Southern-Style Raw Kibbeh

*Frakeh*

*Frakeh* is made with a special southern spice mix called *kamouneh*. I have included the recipe because once you start using this spice blend, you won't stop. If you have a garden, use your own dried herbs, or buy them from a local spice shop where you are sure that you are getting fresh ones. Women who make *frakeh* in the traditional way will pound fresh meat with salt on a marble slab set on the ground using a wooden pestle. The best way to eat *frakeh* is to sit with someone who is making it (preferably a smiling mother figure) and, while you watch the ritual unravel before your eyes, open your mouth to receive small tastes wrapped in bread from her hands. I speak from experience. Thank you Zeinab!

½ small onion, quartered

1 scallion, trimmed

A few sprigs of fresh flat-leaf parsley

A few sprigs of fresh marjoram

A few sprigs of fresh basil

A few sprigs of fresh mint

½ teaspoon orange zest

½ hot chile pepper (optional)

3 tablespoons fine brown bulgur

1 teaspoon southern spice mix
   (*kamouneh*, see facing page)

Pinch salt

5½ oz (150 g) very fresh ground
   lamb tenderloin or ground
   beef sirloin

Ice cubes

Extra-virgin olive oil

In a food processor, combine the onion, scallion, parsley, marjoram, basil, mint, orange zest, and chile, if using, and process until pureed. Mix in the bulgur, 1 teaspoon of spice mix, and salt. Set aside in a mixing bowl.

Put the meat in the freezer for 30 minutes before processing for best results. Should it be impossible for you to freeze the meat in advance, you can add 2 ice cubes as you work. Put the meat into the food processor, add a pinch of salt, and begin processing at a low speed. Gradually increase the speed until the meat is finely ground with a cream-like consistency. Run a knife through it to gather any impurities. Add the meat to the seasoned bulgur mixture in the bowl.

Moistening your hands with cold water to prevent sticking, knead the mixture with your hands until well mixed.

To serve, you can flatten the mixture on a plate to about 1 in (2 cm) thick, making grooves in the surface for the olive oil. Alternatively, use moistened hands to divide the meat into bite-size portions and form elongated balls. Squeeze each slightly to make indentations in the mixture with your fingers and arrange them on a serving dish. Serve immediately or keep in the fridge for 30 minutes, at most. Drizzle with olive oil just before serving with Arabic bread. Any leftovers can be cooked.

# Southern Spice Mix
*Kamouneh*

MAKES ABOUT 3 TABLESPOONS

1 tablespoon cumin seeds
1½ teaspoons black peppercorns
1 teaspoon allspice berries
1 tablespoon dried edible
   rose petals (optional)
2 teaspoons dried marjoram
1 teaspoon dried basil
1 teaspoon dried mint
1 clove
Pinch ground nutmeg
1 bay leaf

Combine all of the ingredients in a spice grinder. Transfer to an airtight jar and store in a cool dark place for up to a year.

# Baked Kibbeh

## *Kibbeh bi Saniyeh*

In this dish, kibbeh shell and stuffing mixture are layered and baked in a dish—meatloaf, the Lebanese way! It is often served with a cooling cucumber-yogurt dip called *Laban wa Khyar*, but you can also serve it with a simple green salad.

1 large onion, quartered

1 lb (450 g) lean ground lamb
  or beef

½ teaspoon ground allspice

¼ teaspoon ground cinnamon
  (optional)

¼ teaspoon freshly ground
  black pepper

½ teaspoon salt

Ice cubes

3 cups (500 g) fine brown bulgur

½ cup (120 ml) vegetable oil

4 tablespoons butter

Yogurt with Cucumbers
  (*Laban wa Khyar*, see facing
  page), to serve (optional)

### STUFFING

2 tablespoons clarified butter
  or butter

½ cup (70 g) pine nuts

3 large onions, finely chopped

1 lb (450 g) ground lamb tenderloin
  or ground beef sirloin

1 teaspoon ground allspice

1 teaspoon salt

To make the kibbeh shell mixture: Finely chop the onion in a food processor. Add the ground meat, along with the spices and salt and a couple of ice cubes. Blend until you have a smooth, creamy paste. Wash and drain the bulgur well, then add it to the meat mixture. Pulse for 1 minute to combine. Transfer to a mixing bowl. Prepare a small bowl of ice water. Dipping your hands into the ice water periodically to prevent sticking, knead the mixture for a few minutes until smooth and uniform.

To make the stuffing: Melt 1 tablespoon of the clarified butter in a frying pan. Sauté the pine nuts until golden brown, watching carefully so they don't burn. Remove with a slotted spoon and set aside on paper towels to drain. Add the rest of the clarified butter to the pan and sauté the onions until translucent. Stir in the ground meat, allspice, and salt, and cook, breaking up the meat with a wooden spoon, until well browned, 8 to 10 minutes. Once cooked, stir in the fried pine nuts and set aside.

Grease the bottom of a 12 in (30 cm) round baking dish with ¼ cup (60 ml) of the vegetable oil. Preheat the oven to 400°F (200°C).

With moistened hands, divide the shell mixture into two portions, then form each part into 4 even pieces to make 8. Spread 4 pieces in the base of the baking dish, flattening them to form an even layer about 1 in (2.5 cm) thick. Spread the stuffing evenly over the base. Repeat the process with the remaining 4 pieces to cover the stuffing, smoothing the surface.

Moisten a sharp knife with cold water, then pass the tip of the knife around the edges of the dish to push the kibbeh away from the sides. Cut the kibbeh into diamond-shaped serving pieces and score the top to make a geometric design, if you wish. Poke a hole in the center with your finger.

In a small saucepan, melt the butter with the remaining vegetable oil and pour or brush it evenly over the kibbeh. Bake for 20 to 25 minutes, until cooked through and golden on top. Serve the kibbeh warm or at room temperature with *Laban wa Khyar* or a simple green salad.

# Yogurt with Cucumbers    SERVES 6 TO 8
*Laban wa Khyar*

8 oz (225 g) Lebanese or Persian
   cucumbers, peeled and sliced
2 cups (450 g) plain yogurt
1 tablespoon crumbled dried mint
½ teaspoon salt, or to taste
1 garlic clove, peeled and crushed
   (optional)

Combine all of the ingredients in a bowl and taste for seasoning. Set aside
in the refrigerator until served.

# Kibbeh in Yogurt Sauce

## *Kibbeh Labaniyeh*

Kibbeh cooked in yogurt (*laban*) is a family favorite eaten throughout the country. Some families serve this dish on New Year's Day to start the year with a clean slate—the white sauce is emblematic of purity. This recipe may have originated in the Bekaa Valley, where cow milk is abundant. In the Chouf, the yogurt sauce is enriched with *Awarma* (Lebanese Lamb Confit, p. 197), making a hearty variation that is especially good during the cold winter months. Some families add slow-cooked veal and its broth as well. In the mountains of Lebanon, goat milk yogurt is used instead of cow milk, giving the dish a pungent, tangier flavor (goat milk doesn't separate during cooking, and some find it easier to digest). If you have a store of Kibbeh Balls (p. 106) in your freezer, this dish comes together quickly—they can be fried, baked, or boiled before adding them to the stew.

4 cups (1 kg) plain, full-fat cow or
   goat yogurt
12 kibbeh balls (p. 106), stuffed or
   left hollow, uncooked, fried,
   or frozen (see method)
1 large egg, whisked (if using cow
   milk yogurt)
1½ tablespoon cornstarch diluted
   with ¼ cup (120 ml) water
2 tablespoons extra-virgin olive oil
2–3 garlic cloves, minced
1 bunch mint or cilantro, leaves
   finely chopped, or 1 tablespoon
   dried mint, crumbled

An hour before you cook the yogurt sauce, it is best to bring out the yogurt from the refrigerator and let it stand at room temperature.

Prepare your kibbeh balls: If they are raw or frozen, you can deep-fry them (see p. 107), bake them in an oven preheated to 400°F (200°C) for 5 minutes, or drop them in a pot of boiling water for 2 minutes (remove with a slotted spoon and pierce them in a few places with a toothpick—this will help them hold their shape).

Put the yogurt in a saucepan and set over medium heat. Add the egg (if using) and salt, and slowly bring to a boil, whisking constantly in the same direction to prevent the yogurt from curdling (egg helps with this). As soon as the yogurt starts to bubble, lower the heat to a gentle simmer and whisk in the cornstarch water. Simmer, whisking constantly, for 10 minutes, until the sauce has thickened.

Drop the kibbeh balls gently into the hot yogurt and simmer for another 10 minutes, stirring carefully so they don't break.

Meanwhile, in a small frying pan, heat the olive oil over medium heat and garlic sauté the garlic just until golden. Mix in the mint or cilantro, lower the heat, and cook just until the leaves have wilted, but are still green. Gently stir into the yogurt sauce.

Serve hot, with plain rice, or Vermicelli Rice (p. 177).

# Kibbeh with Citrus Tahini Sauce

*Kibbeh Arnabiyeh*

In this dish, kibbeh balls and chunks of slow-cooked lamb or beef are served in a creamy sauce made with tahini and citrus juice. Tradition dictates that the recipe should contain up to seven citrus juices, including orange, bitter orange, grapefruit, tangerine, mandarin, and lemon, so feel free to try your favorite combination. The kibbeh balls can be fried, baked, or boiled before adding them to the sauce.

1 lb (450 g) boneless lamb shank or beef chuck, cut into chunks

1 tablespoon coarse sea salt

1–2 bay leaves

1 cinnamon stick

6 onions, 1 quartered, 5 sliced

12 kibbeh balls (p. 106), stuffed or left hollow, uncooked, fried, or frozen (see below)

1¼ cups (200 g) drained cooked or canned chickpeas

4 tablespoons extra-virgin olive oil

### CITRUS TAHINI SAUCE

1 cup (240 g) tahini

⅔ cup (150 ml) freshly squeezed bitter orange juice or grapefruit juice

¼ cup (60 ml) freshly squeezed orange juice

¼ cup (60 ml) freshly squeezed lemon juice

¼ teaspoon orange zest

1 teaspoon salt

¼ teaspoon ground white pepper

2–3 drops orange blossom water

Place the lamb in a large pot and cover with water. Bring to a boil, skimming the foam that forms on the surface. Reduce the heat to a simmer and add the salt, bay leaves, cinnamon stick, and quartered onion. Cover the pot and simmer for about 50 minutes until the lamb is very tender. Top up the water, if needed, to keep the meat covered during cooking. Strain the broth and set the meat and broth aside. Discard the bay leaves, cinnamon, and onion.

Prepare your kibbeh balls: If they are raw or frozen, you can deep-fry them (as on p. 107), bake them in an oven preheated to 400°F (200°C) for 5 minutes, or drop them in a pot of boiling water for 2 minutes (remove with a slotted spoon and pierce them in a few places with a toothpick—this will help them hold their shape).

Make the sauce: In a mixing bowl, whisk the tahini with the citrus juices, orange zest, salt, and pepper until combined.

Heat the oil in a large sauté pan over medium heat, and sauté the sliced onions until golden. Add the chickpeas, citrus mixture, meat, and 2 cups (475 ml) of the reserved broth. Lower the heat and simmer until the sauce has thickened, about 10 minutes.

Drop the kibbeh balls gently into the sauce and simmer for another 10 minutes, stirring gently from time to time to make sure you don't break them. When ready, you will see the oil from the tahini start to separate. Remove from the heat and stir in the orange blossom water to finish.

Serve hot, with rice or Vermicelli Rice (p. 177).

# Northern-Style Kibbeh

## *Kibbeh Zghartawiyeh*

One of the most famous kibbeh dishes in Lebanon is from Zgharta, a city in the north of Lebanon, where locals take great pride in sharing this food with city folks. The kibbeh is shaped in a glass bowl to form them in the shape of an inflated ball. It is traditionally stuffed with minced sheep fat and grilled over charcoal—robust mountain food at its best, but not for the faint-hearted. You need lean ground meat for the shell mixture; if you can't find this, use lamb shank, trimmed of its fat and coarsely ground.

1 large onion, quartered

1 lb (450 g) lean ground lamb
  or beef

½ teaspoon ground allspice

¼ teaspoon ground cinnamon
  (optional)

¼ teaspoon freshly ground
  black pepper

½ teaspoon salt

Ice cubes

2½ cups (400 g) fine brown bulgur

Vegetable oil, for brushing

**STUFFING**

5 oz (150 g) goat or lamb fat,
  cut into chunks

1 small onion

¼ bunch flat-leaf parsley,
  finely chopped

3 mint sprigs, leaves stripped and
  finely chopped (optional)

½ teaspoon salt

½ teaspoon red pepper flakes
  (optional)

To make the kibbeh shell mixture: Finely chop the onion in a food processor. Add the ground meat, along with the spices and salt and a couple of ice cubes. Blend until you have a smooth, creamy paste. Wash and drain the bulgur well, then add it to the meat mixture. Pulse for 1 minute to combine. Transfer to a mixing bowl. Prepare a bowl of ice water. Dipping your hands into the water periodically to prevent sticking, knead the mixture for a few minutes until smooth and uniform. Divide into 12 portions and set aside.

To make the stuffing: Freeze the fat for 30 minutes to firm up. Grind in a food processor or meat grinder, along with the remaining stuffing ingredients until combined and coarsely ground.

To mold the kibbeh: Lightly oil a baking tray. Wet a sheet of thick plastic wrap with water and use it to line a 5 in (12 cm) round glass bowl. Wetting your hands as you work, press a portion of the meat dough into the bowl, pushing it around until it is evenly about ¼ in (6 mm) thick, lining the bowl. Carefully use the plastic to remove the shell from the bowl. Place on the oiled tray and peel off the plastic. Repeat, wetting your hands with cold water as you work. Every 2 molds will make one kibbeh.

Fill one mold with 2 tablespoons of the stuffing. Place another mold on top and press to seal. Cut away excess mixture at the joint using your fingers or a sharp knife, and place on the oiled tray. Brush the surface with vegetable oil. For best results, freeze for 30 minutes to an hour before grilling, so the kibbeh hold their shape.

Heat a gas or charcoal grill to medium. Grill the kibbeh, turning them periodically, for 30 to 35 minutes, or until evenly browned. Serve hot, cutting through the ball horizontally to avoid the fat spilling out.

# Fish Kibbeh, Two Ways

## *Kibbet Samak*

If one dish could sum up the flavors of the Mediterranean Sea and the Lebanese coast, it would have to be fish kibbeh. This recipe is versatile, as you can choose to deep-fry them as balls, or layer the shell and stuffing mixture in a baking dish as in Baked Kibbeh (p. 116), and bake it in the oven.

1 lb (450 g) white fish fillets, such as cod, haddock, hake, or halibut, cut into chunks

1 onion, quartered

½ teaspoon lemon zest

½ teaspoon orange zest

1 bunch cilantro, stems removed

2 teaspoons ground coriander

½ teaspoon ground allspice

½ teaspoon ground cumin

1 teaspoon salt

½ teaspoon ground white pepper

Ice cubes

1¾ cups (300 g) fine white bulgur

Vegetable oil, for frying, or olive oil, for drizzling

*Continued on next page*

To make the kibbeh shell mixture: In a large bowl, combine the fish, onion, lemon and orange zests, spices, salt, and white pepper and mix well. Use a meat grinder (preferably) or food processor to grind the mixture finely. Pulse until ground, but not puréed; you are aiming for a dough-like consistency. Return to the bowl and prepare a bowl of ice water.

Wash the bulgur and drain well, squeezing out excess moisture. Mix the bulgur into the fish mixture. With moistened hands to prevent sticking, knead the mixture for a few minutes until smooth and uniform. If you find the mixture to be too stiff, add a little bit of water, a tablespoon at a time, until you have a pliable consistency. Set aside.

Next, make the stuffing: Boil the lemon and orange peels in a pot of water for 15 minutes. Drain in a colander, rinse, and drain. Taste, repeating the process if they are still bitter. Set aside.

Heat 1 tablespoon of the olive oil in a frying pan. Sauté the pine nuts until they turn golden brown. Remove with a slotted spoon and set aside on stacked paper towels. Add another tablespoon of olive oil to the pan and fry the sliced onions until soft with salt, white pepper, and Aleppo pepper or cayenne, if using. Stir in the saffron water and simmer for about 3 minutes to infuse. Remove from heat and stir in the boiled citrus peels and the pine nuts. Transfer to a bowl.

Now you must decide whether you would like to make fried kibbeh balls, or a baked kibbeh dish.

For fried kibbeh balls: Moisten your hands with the cold water, divide the shell mixture into even balls each about the size of a walnut. Place one ball in your hand. Poke a hole in the ball using the index finger of your other hand, and rotate your finger to make a hollow. The walls of the shell should be an even ½ in (1 cm) thick and the length about 3 in (8 cm). Be careful not pierce the bottom or sides of the shell. Spoon about 2 teaspoons of the stuffing into the hollow and pinch the opening together with moistened fingers to

## STUFFING

1 large lemon peel, pith removed, sliced into very thin strips

1 large orange peel, pith removed, sliced into very thin strips

2 tablespoons extra-virgin olive oil

½ cup (70 g) pine nuts

2 large onions, sliced

1 teaspoon salt

¼ teaspoon white pepper

½ teaspoon Aleppo pepper or cayenne (optional)

1 teaspoon saffron, steeped in 1 cup (240 ml) hot water

## TO SERVE (OPTIONAL)

Tahini sauce (*tarator*, p. 68)

1 onion, sliced and fried until golden

Lemon wedges

seal the opening, forming the kibbeh into a football shape. Repeat with the remaining shell mixture and stuffing. At this stage, you can freeze them (first spaced out on a tray, then in sealed containers or bags), or proceed to frying.

Pour vegetable oil into a large pot or deep-fryer to a depth of 2 in (5 cm). Heat until the oil reaches a temperature of 350°F (180°C), or until small bubbles gather around a small piece of bread dropped into the oil. Working in batches, deep-fry the kibbeh for 3–4 minutes until golden brown on all sides. Using a slotted spoon, transfer to a colander to drain excess oil.

For baked kibbeh: Grease the bottom of a 12 in (30 cm) round baking dish with ¼ cup (60 ml) of vegetable oil. Preheat the oven to 400°F (200°C).

With moistened hands, divide the kibbeh into two portions, then form each portion into 4 pieces to make 8. Spread 4 pieces in the base of the baking dish, flattening them to form an even layer about 1 in (2.5 cm) thick. Spread the stuffing evenly over the base. Repeat the process with the remaining 4 pieces of shell mixture to cover the stuffing, smoothing the surface. Moisten a sharp knife with cold water, then pass the tip of the knife deeply around the edges of the dish to push the kibbeh away from the sides. Then cut the kibbeh into diamond-shaped serving pieces, scoring the top to make a geometric design, if you wish. Drizzle with a little olive oil, if you like, and bake for 20 to 25 minutes, until cooked through and golden.

Serve warm or at room temperature with *tarator* mixed with fried onion, if you wish, and lemon wedges alongside.

# GRILLS

# GRILLS

## *Mashawi*

Everything tastes better outdoors. Lebanese love to grill meats, poultry, and fish on an open fire. Family and friends gather around the barbecue, as the designated person grills meats to perfection. If left unnoticed for a split second, the meat is overcooked and spoils the meal. It certainly takes skill and practice.

In our house in the mountains, we gather thick branches and sticks from our backyard to feed the fire. The house is overrun by large rosemary bushes, which I trim every year. The thick branches of dried rosemary leaves add a delicious scent to our grills. We even thread the meat onto thin branches of rosemary instead of skewers. My husband, like most Lebanese men, is responsible for the actual grilling.

The marinade plays an important role to get full flavors. It is best to plan when you want to grill, as most meats need to be marinated overnight for the best flavor. This is the rule, but rules are very often broken. There are times when we decide to grill on the spot, and I have had success in marinating meats for just a few hours. Luckily in Lebanon, most butchers will sell marinated meat and poultry to customers. All that is needed is to thread them onto a skewer, adding a few vegetables to the mix. Often when I go out on my balcony in Beirut on Sundays, I can smell neighbors grilling their meal on a "*manqal*"—a portable metal grill.

Every traditional restaurant in Lebanon serving mezze has a grilling station. Grilled meats, poultry, and seafood (*mashawi*) are served as a second course after all the small plates have been wiped clean. Sometimes, diners will skip this part as they are so full, yet most can't resist continuing.

Many city dwellers visit the countryside on weekends to eat at local restaurants. Our family has been doing it for years with friends. I remember once we arrived at a small family-owned restaurant craving mezze and grilled meats. The owner, delighted to see such a crowd, told us that the meat could be served but would need a bit more time than usual. We agreed because we were famished. He showed us a goat tied to a pole and said, "Here we serve the meat fresh." Two hours later, we were served *lahm meshwi*—grilled meat on skewers. It was certainly an unforgettable experience.

It is very convenient to make a spice box to use in marinades or simply for cooking Lebanese food. I use recycled metal boxes to make several compartments. You can be creative and buy old containers or jars in a thrift shop to make your personalized spice box. I arrange the boxes in a larger metal box, then fill them as needed. Keep the lids, as they will keep your spices fresh and help them last longer. My spice box includes cinnamon sticks, dried bay leaves, ground cinnamon, allspice, Lebanese 7-spice (*baharat*), black pepper, white pepper, cumin, sumac, and ground chile pepper. You can add more or less to the box, depending on which spices you use more often. This selection is a good base to start with.

**Left:** Building a close relationship with one's butcher is important. If you befriend him, he will give you the finest cuts of meat and advise you on which meat to use for your recipe.

# Grilled Chicken Skewers with Garlic Sauce

## Shish Taouk

The secret to delicious *shish taouk* is good quality meat and the flavorful marinade—which is either white or vibrant red. *Toum* (a creamy garlic sauce) gives the dish its distinctive flavor, and is used both to flavor the marinade, and as a dipping sauce at the table. My husband, Serge, and I often order *shish taouk* sandwiches from our popular neighborhood spot, Kababji, whenever we have a craving. Serge will always ask, *"taouk ma' toum allil"* (light on the garlic sauce), and is always disappointed in the flavor without the garlic kick. The garlic sauce may be strong, but it makes the whole experience worthwhile. As my father would say, eating *shish taouk* without extra *toum* is *"mitel hadan am bi bouss ekhto"* like kissing one's sister—an old Lebanese saying.

Shishk taouk is typically served as part of a barbecue meal, tucked inside a pocket of Arabic bread, or sometimes with *Khubzeh Harra* (Spicy Topped Flatbread, p. 133), on a serving plate. The bread soaks up the juices and can be used to hold the chicken to slide it off the skewers. *Shish taouk* sandwiches are made in Arabic bread, with grilled chicken and vegetables, lettuce, pickles, a few fries, and of course a spoonful of garlic sauce. Before you start, choose whether you are making the white (yogurt) marinade, or the red (tomato) marinade.

Juice of 1–2 lemons

¼ cup (60 ml) extra-virgin olive oil

1 teaspoon dried oregano

1 teaspoon salt

½ teaspoon ground white pepper

2¼ lb (1 kg) boneless chicken breasts or thighs, cut into chunks

Handful of cherry tomatoes or quartered tomatoes (optional)

Handful of peeled pearl onions or onion slices (optional)

Arabic bread (p. 28), to serve

**WHITE MARINADE**

1 teaspoon lemon zest

4 tablespoons plain yogurt

*Continued on next page*

Make the garlic sauce: In a small jug, combine the lemon juice and crushed ice. Place garlic in a small food processor with salt and blend until it is finely minced. Scrape down the sides. With the processor running, start pouring the oil very slowly in a thin stream. When the mixture starts to become airy and emulsifies, begin to alternate the oil with the cold lemon juice. The process should take 10 to 15 minutes, for best results.

In a large mixing bowl, combine lemon juice, olive oil, ½ cup (100 g) of the garlic sauce, and the oregano, salt, and pepper. Then add either the yogurt marinade ingredients, or the tomato marinade ingredients. Whisk well, add the chicken, and stir to coat with the marinade. Marinate in the refrigerator overnight or for at least two hours.

If you are using wooden skewers, soak them in cold water for 30 minutes. Prepare a gas or charcoal grill. Thread the chicken pieces onto skewers, alternating them with cherry tomatoes and pearl onions, if you like. Grill over medium heat, turning the skewers, until the chicken is lightly charred and cooked through, 12 to 15 minutes, depending on your grill. Open up a round of Arabic bread and tuck the cooked chicken into it on a plate. Serve hot, with the remaining garlic sauce on the side. (Also pictured on p. 126.)

## RED MARINADE

1 tablespoon tomato paste

1 teaspoon red pepper paste
  (p. 200)

## GARLIC SAUCE (*TOUM*)

3 tablespoons freshly squeezed
  lemon juice

¾ cup (100 g) crushed ice

6 large garlic cloves, peeled

1 teaspoon salt

2 cups (450 ml) vegetable oil

# Grilled Lamb Skewers with Spicy Flatbread

*Laham Meshwi ma' Khubzeh Harra*

Come spring, when the weather changes, wildflowers bloom all over Lebanon. Families and friends take advantage of sunny weekends to plan picnics in country villages outside of the city. People of all ages will dust off the *manqal*, a portable metal barbecue, to grill meats outside. Marinated meats, salads, potatoes, and cold drinks are transported in neat packages in the back of the car with the *manqal*. The meal is made with few ingredients and basic equipment, but there is always a festive, convivial atmosphere to the shared ritual. Most Lebanese have a trusted source for buying the freshest meats for grilling, and many butcher shops even advertise ready-made marinated meats for convenience. This dish of grilled marinated meat and vegetables is most often served with *Khubzeh Harra*, a spicy topped flatbread that perfectly complements the smoky flavors.

½ teaspoon ground allspice

1 teaspoon salt

¼ teaspoon ground black pepper

¼ teaspoon cayenne

1 teaspoon dried rosemary needles or oregano, crushed

2–3 firm red tomatoes, sliced

1 medium onion, sliced

1 lemon, cut into wedges

3 tablespoons red wine vinegar

¼ cup (60 ml) vegetable oil

¼ cup (60 ml) extra-virgin olive oil

2¼ lb (1 kg) lamb or beef tenderloin, cut into chunks

1 small piece of lamb or beef fat for each skewer

Handful of cherry tomatoes and/or

Handful of peeled pearl onions

1–2 green bell peppers, quartered

Spicy Topped Flatbread (*Khubzeh Harra*, see facing page), to serve

In a large mixing bowl, combine the spices, tomatoes, onions, and lemon wedges. Pour in the vinegar and oils and mix well. Add the meat and fat and stir to coat well with the marinade. Marinate in the refrigerator overnight or for at least 4 hours. Remove from the refrigerator at least 30 minutes before you plan to grill. If using wooden skewers, soak them in cold water for 30 minutes before using.

Preheat a gas or charcoal grill. Thread the meat and fat evenly onto skewers, alternating the pieces with cherry tomatoes, pepper slices, and pearl onions; or you can thread the vegetables onto separate skewers. Discard the remaining marinade.

Ready your *Khubzeh Harra*, then grill the skewers over medium heat, turning them for even cooking, for 12 to 15 minutes, until the meat is cooked to your liking and is lightly charred at the edges.

# Spicy Topped Flatbread   MAKES 2

*Khubzeh Harra*

2 large Arabic breads (p. 28)
1 tablespoon tomato paste
½ teaspoon red pepper paste (p. 200)
1½ tablespoons extra-virgin olive oil
2 tomatoes, finely chopped
1 red onion, sliced
1 tablespoon ground sumac
Handful chopped parsley

In a bowl, mix the tomato paste, red pepper paste, and olive oil and spread the mixture onto the darker side of each bread. In another bowl, mix the tomatoes, onion, and sumac. Place the bread on the grill (light side down) to warm through, then top with the tomatoes, onion, and sumac and remove from the grill. Sprinkle with chopped parsley. The bread can be cut like a pie to serve with the meat, or you can tuck the meat within a pocket to serve. (Pictured overleaf.)

# Ground Meat Skewers with Parsley and Onion

## *Kafta*

*Kafta* is a simple ground meat skewer, made with ground beef or lamb flavored with onion, parsley, and spices. There are a few rules though to follow. The first rule is to use meat with a high fat content so the kebab is tender, juicy, and full of flavor—in Lebanon, we even add additional lamb fat. The second rule is to cut the parsley by hand using a sharp knife. Using a food processor will yield wet parsley, which will impact the texture. The third and final rule is not to overcook the meat, to avoid it drying out. (If you are cooking indoors, you can form the mixture into patties and cook them in a frying pan as you would burgers. You can serve *kafta* in a pocket of Arabic bread, or in *Khubzeh Harra* (Spicy Topped Flatbread, p. 133). Follow these tips and enjoy the final result.

1 lb (450 g) ground beef with 20% fat

2 oz (50 g) lamb fat (optional)

1 medium onion, very finely chopped

½ teaspoon ground allspice

1 teaspoon salt

Pinch freshly ground black pepper

1 small bunch flat-leaf parsley, finely chopped by hand

Arabic bread (p. 28), to serve (optional)

If you can, ask your butcher to coarsely grind the meat with the fat, or use a food processor to pulse them together briefly, just until mixed.

In a mixing bowl, combine the chopped onion, allspice, salt, and pepper. Place the meat on a clean work surface and mix in the chopped parsley and onion mixture. Knead until you have a homogeneous dough-like consistency.

Prepare a small bowl of water for moistening your hands while you handle the meat. With moistened hands, divide the mixture into about 10 even pieces, and roll them into balls. Put one ball in the palm of your hand. Use the other hand, push a flat skewer into the ball and squeeze to form the ball into a sausage shape about 1½ inches (4 cm) thick around the skewer. Taper the ends and suspend the skewer over a baking pan or rack, ready to grill. Repeat with the remaining pieces.

Preheat a gas or charcoal grill. Grill over medium heat, turning the skewers, until the meat is cooked to your liking and lightly charred at the edges, 5 to 7 minutes. Open up a round of Arabic bread, place on a serving dish, and tuck the meat inside.

# Aleppo Kebab

*Kebab Halabi*

I come from a multinational family: My maternal grandmother was from Aleppo, Syria, and married my grandfather who was French. My paternal grandmother was born in the US to Armenian parents who fled Turkey, and she married my Lebanese grandfather. As a child I had the feeling that there were too many identities to relate to, so I completely ignored my Syrian and Armenian heritage. Today, I feel quite the opposite. As a young wife and mother of three children, I had the opportunity to visit Aleppo with a group of friends before the war broke out. It was a revelation; Not only did I instantly feel a certain belonging to the city, but I was fascinated by the food, especially the meat dishes. I had never tasted such high-quality meats. I am generally more inclined to eat vegetarian dishes, but this was not the case in Aleppo. Aleppo's cuisine is legendary, and there are numerous varieties of kebab. This one is my interpretation of a dish I tasted on that visit. If you can, ask your butcher to grind the beef with 2 oz (50 g) of lamb fat for even more flavor.

1 medium onion, very finely chopped

1 teaspoon ground cumin

1 teaspoon Aleppo pepper, cayenne, or paprika, plus extra to garnish

1 tablespoon red pepper paste (p. 200)

1½ teaspoons salt

¼ teaspoon freshly ground black pepper

1 lb (450 g) ground beef with 20% fat

½ cup (50 g) coarsely chopped pistachios (optional)

½ cup (125 g) plain yogurt

**TOMATO SAUCE**

1 tablespoon extra-virgin olive oil

1 large onion, sliced

1 red bell pepper, sliced

2 large tomatoes, peeled, diced

1 teaspoon salt

1 tablespoon ground sumac

In a mixing bowl, combine the chopped onion, cumin, Aleppo pepper, red pepper paste, salt, and pepper. Place the meat on a clean work surface and mix in the onion mixture and pistachios. Knead until you have a homogeneous dough-like consistency. Set aside.

Make the sauce: Heat the oil in a frying pan over medium heat and sauté the onion until golden. Add the bell pepper, tomatoes, and salt. Cook for about 5 minutes, until the tomatoes and peppers soften. Sprinkle with the sumac. Set aside.

Prepare a small bowl of water for moistening your hands while you handle the meat. With moistened hands, divide the kebab mixture into about 10 even pieces and roll them into balls. Put one ball in the palm of your hand. Use the other hand, push a flat skewer into the ball and squeeze to form a sausage shape, about 1½ inches (4 cm) thick, around the skewer. Taper the ends and suspend the skewer over a baking pan or rack, ready to grill. Repeat with the remaining pieces.

Preheat a gas or charcoal grill. Grill over medium heat, turning the skewers, until the meat is cooked to your liking and lightly charred at the edges, 5 to 7 minutes.

If needed, warm the sauce and transfer to a large serving dish. Top with the grilled kebabs, then pour the yogurt on top. Sprinkle with a little Aleppo pepper and serve hot, with Arabic bread (p. 28).

# Grilled Lamb Chops

*Kastalleta Ghanam Meshwi*

Lamb chops are the most expensive cuts of meat, as they are the most delicious and tender choice. Taken from the ribs of the lamb, they are cooked individually over the grill for just a few minutes. They simply melt in your mouth. My food philosophy has always been to focus on quality instead of quantity—good for the earth, good for the body. A few chops served at a family barbeque will leave a lasting impression. Last summer, I invited my in-laws to a last-minute lunch in the backyard. I had prepared skewers of chicken and meat for the occasion with a big bowl of *fattoush* (p. 16), and Belgian fries (more about that later). As we ate, I gave my husband, the designated grill master, a few lamb chops that I had marinated the day before. He grilled them for a few minutes and served them proudly to his parents. Jacqueline, my Belgian mother-in-law (hence the Belgian fries) is a meat connoisseur and was wowed by these. A no-fuss recipe with great results!

8 lamb rib chops

2 teaspoons salt

1 teaspoon freshly ground
   black pepper

½ teaspoon dried wild thyme
   or oregano

A few sprigs of fresh herbs (basil,
   dill, cilantro, sage, rosemary,
   chives, or parsley), chopped

5–7 garlic cloves, sliced

Pinch Aleppo pepper or crushed
   red pepper flakes

5 tablespoons extra-virgin olive oil

Season the lamb chops on both sides with salt and pepper.

In a mixing bowl, combine the dried and fresh herbs, garlic, and Aleppo pepper. Pour in the olive oil and mix well. Add the lamb chops and rub the marinade into them to evenly coat them. Marinate in the refrigerator overnight, or for at least 4 hours. Remove from the fridge at least 30 minutes before grilling.

Prepare a gas or charcoal grill. Grill over high heat for 2 minutes on each side, or until browned but still pink in the middle. Remove from the heat and leave to rest for 5 minutes before serving.

# Whole Grilled Chicken

## *Farrouj Meshwi*

Plan ahead before you make this recipe. The marinade plays the most important role to give you tender and juicy grilled chicken. Choose the grill master wisely as you don't want the chicken to be under- or overcooked. It needs to be just right. This takes experience, like all things in life. I often rely on my senses and intuition to know when food is ready, a debate I have often with my husband and son (the chef). They rely more on timers and the science behind cooking techniques. I guess I am old-fashioned, using all my senses to determine the outcome. Who's right, who's wrong; who's to say? Carlo Petrini, founder of the international Slow Food movement, visited me in Lebanon a few years ago. Before leaving he said to me, "I came to Lebanon to meet a real Italian mama." *Capito*? Mamas use their maternal instincts when cooking.

1 large free-range chicken
   (about 5 lb/2.25 kg)
3 garlic cloves
4 tablespoons freshly squeezed
   lemon juice
½ cup (120 ml) vegetable oil
Pinch Aleppo pepper or cayenne
¼ teaspoon ground cinnamon
¼ teaspoon ground allspice
¼ teaspoon ground cumin
2 tablespoons garlic sauce (*toum*,
   p. 130), plus extra to serve
1 tablespoon red pepper paste
   (p. 200, optional)
Arabic bread (p. 28), to serve
Salt

**MARINADE**

2 garlic cloves, crushed
1½ tablespoon freshly squeezed
   lemon juice
1 tablespoon ground sumac
2 tablespoons extra-virgin olive oil

Ask your butcher to butterfly the chicken, or do it yourself: Place the chicken on a cutting board, backbone facing you. Use kitchen shears to cut along both sides of the spine. Remove the backbone and push down on the breasts to flatten the chicken. Turn it over and remove the wingtips.

Pat dry with paper towels and season the chicken all over with salt. Gently lift the skin to apply salt underneath.

Crush the garlic with a pinch of salt in a mortar and pestle. In a large dish, combine the crushed garlic, lemon juice, oil, spices, garlic sauce, and red pepper paste (if using). Place the chicken in the bowl and coat well in the marinade, rubbing it into the flesh. Lay the chicken flat with the skin side up. Marinate in the refrigerator overnight or for at least 4 hours. Remove from the refrigerator at least 30 minutes before grilling.

Prepare the sauce for basting by pouring the leftover marinade into a jar. Close the lid and shake it. Set aside.

Prepare a gas or charcoal grill so that you have a hotter side and a cooler side. Start by placing the chicken skin side up on the grill over medium-high indirect heat. Brushing with the marinade periodically, grill the chicken for 45 minutes to 1 hour, or until the internal temperature reaches 165°F (75°C). To finish, flip the chicken over onto the hotter side of your grill to char and crisp the skin.

Remove the chicken from the heat and wrap it in Arabic bread. Set aside to rest for 5 minutes before serving, with garlic sauce on the side.

# Chicken Shawarma

## *Shawarma Djej*

Shawarma, a common street food in Lebanon, refers to a method of cooking marinated chicken or meat on a vertical spit that rotates in front of a fire or a scorching heat source. The meat slowly cooks while the spit rotates. The operator will shave off tender pieces as it roasts, quickly serving customers. Chicken shawarma is served wrapped in a pocket of Arabic bread with tomatoes, lettuce, garlic sauce (*toum*) or hummus, pickles, and a few French fries. In Beirut, students line up at the nearest shawarma joint for a quick meal. Lavish Lebanese weddings with elaborate buffets now often have a grilling station for bite-size shawarma. I always get a kick out of seeing the large line of people in their finery patiently waiting for a bite of shawarma served in a tiny pocket of bread. You can reproduce the taste of chicken shawarma at home using this recipe.

1 large onion, sliced

3–4 garlic cloves, sliced

1 lemon peel, sliced

1 teaspoon salt

½ teaspoon ground white pepper

½ teaspoon ground mastic
  (Arabic gum, see p. 216), optional

1 teaspoon ground oregano

½ teaspoon ground cardamom,
  or 2 cardamom pods, toasted
  and crushed

¼ teaspoon ground cinnamon

½ teaspoon ground coriander

¼ teaspoon ground cumin

4 tablespoons vegetable oil,
  plus extra for greasing

5 tablespoons freshly squeezed
  lemon juice

1 tablespoon red pepper paste
  (p. 200, optional)

2¼ lb (1 kg) boneless skinless
  chicken breasts or thighs

In a large bowl, combine the onion, garlic, lemon peels, salt, and spices. Add the oil, lemon juice, and red pepper paste, if using, and mix well. If you will be oven-baking, cut the chicken breasts or thighs into thin slices; if grilling, keep them whole. Add the chicken to the marinade, and rub until evenly coated. Cover and refrigerate overnight to marinate.

Grill the chicken on your barbecue for 12 to 15 minutes, until cooked through, brushing with the marinade from time to time. Let the chicken rest on a cutting board for 5 minutes, then thinly slice. Alternatively, preheat the oven to 425°F (220°C) and grease a large baking sheet with 1 tablespoon of oil. Arrange the sliced chicken on the baking sheet with its marinade, and bake for 25 to 30 minutes, or until golden and cooked through.

Divide the chicken among the Arabic breads. Top with the *toum* or hummus, tomatoes, lettuce, pickles, and parsley or mint leaves. You can also add a few French fries, if available. Roll it up tightly and serve warm.

*Continued on next page*

**TO SERVE**

Arabic bread (p. 28)

Garlic sauce (*toum*, p. 130)
   or Hummus (p. 52), to serve

3 large tomatoes, sliced

Shredded romaine lettuce

Sliced pickles, such as turnips
   (p. 203), green chile peppers,
   or cucumbers

Coarsely chopped parsley
   or mint leaves

A few French fries (optional)

# Beef or Lamb Shawarma

## *Shawarma Lahmeh*

You don't need a spit oven to make shawarma at home. The secret lies in using the best cut of meat (befriend a butcher, I always say!), and marinating the meat for 12 hours or more. A few years ago, I was a guest chef at the Slow Food University of Gastronomy in Pollenzo, Italy, and I chose to share this flavorful Lebanese street food. Davide, the head chef, patiently baked Arabic bread to give the students the full experience. Students came after lunch to congratulate us. There is nothing in the world more satisfying for a cook than to create bonds and memories through sharing our food traditions.

2 medium onions, sliced

1 bay leaf

1 teaspoon ground cumin

1 teaspoon ground coriander

½ teaspoon paprika

¼ teaspoon ground clove

½ teaspoon cayenne

½ teaspoon freshly ground
   black pepper

½ teaspoon ground cinnamon

1 teaspoon salt

½ cup (120 ml) red wine or vinegar

1 cup (240 ml) vegetable oil,
   plus extra if needed

Peel of 1–2 oranges, thinly sliced

2¼ lb (1 kg) beef sirloin or lamb
   flank steak, thinly sliced

3 large firm tomatoes, sliced

**TO SERVE (OPTIONAL)**

Arabic bread (p. 28)

Tahini sauce (*tarator*, p. 68)

1 onion, sliced

Shredded romaine lettuce

Sliced pickles

Coarsely chopped parsley

In a bowl, combine the onions, spices, salt, wine or vinegar, vegetable oil, and orange peels. Add the meat and mix to coat well. Marinate in the refrigerator for at least 12 hours.

When you are ready to cook, preheat the oven to 425°F (220°C). Using a slotted spoon, remove the meat from marinade and, working in batches if necessary, sear the meat briefly in a hot frying pan with a little oil if necessary, then transfer to a baking dish. Pour the marinade into the baking dish and top with the sliced tomatoes. Bake until cooked to your liking, 15 to 20 minutes.

Serve hot with Arabic bread and plenty of *tarator*. If you want to roll it up into a sandwich, add sliced onion, shredded lettuce, pickles, and parsley and drizzle with tarator.

# Grilled Shrimp

## *Karaydes Meshwi*

One of our favorite pastimes in Lebanon is eating and drinking at seaside restaurants along the coast. Batroun is a coastal city in north Lebanon, and one of the oldest cities in the world; the perfect setting to enjoy fresh seafood specialties. Most of the dishes are simple, relying on the flavor of good quality ingredients, which makes all the difference. In this recipe, like all others, the vital elements are the freshness of the shrimp and the expertise to cook it just right. You can use peeled or unpeeled shrimp in this recipe.

3 garlic cloves

1 teaspoon salt

2–3 scallions, coarsely chopped

½ bunch cilantro, leaves finely
  chopped

2–3 sprigs flat-leaf parsley,
  leaves finely chopped

½ teaspoon white pepper

Juice of 1 lemon

½ cup (120 ml) extra-virgin olive oil

2¼ lb (1 kg) large raw shrimp

Lemon wedges, to serve

Crush the garlic with a pinch of salt in a mortar and pestle. In a mixing bowl, combine the crushed garlic, scallions, cilantro, parsley, and pepper, and then stir in the lemon juice and olive oil. Add the shrimp to the marinade and mix to evenly coat. Refrigerate for 2 hours to marinate.

Prepare a gas or charcoal grill. You can thread the shrimp onto skewers, but it is not necessary; be sure to reserve the marinade. Brushing them frequently with the reserved marinade, grill the shrimp over medium heat for 2–3 minutes per side, just until opaque.

Transfer to a serving dish, garnish with lemon wedges, and serve.

# Grilled Fish

*Samak Meshwi*

Fish can be grilled in so many ways, sometimes with just a simple dressing of lemon and olive oil and a sprinkle of salt. This recipe is more intricate, and full of flavor. My husband employed a man from Syria for many years. He would visit his family often during the year, and on each of these occasions, he would bring us a whole fish, carefully wrapped, as a gift. It was always a joyous event at our house when we received Suleyman's warm token. Our cats rejoiced at the smell of cooking fish too. This recipe is inspired by his, scribbled on a crumpled paper, upon my request. Wrapping the fish in fig leaves makes a neat package for grilling. This is a trick I learned from my good friend Aglaia Kremenzi and her husband Costa in Greece in the beautiful island of Kea, Cyclades (but you can also use foil).

2¼ lb (1 kg) whole white fish, such as sea bass, halibut, red snapper, or cod, scaled and gutted
1 lemon, quartered
Fig leaves or foil, for wrapping
Salt

**STUFFING**

1 medium onion, sliced
1 medium tomato, sliced
4 garlic cloves, sliced
½ bunch flat-leaf parsley, finely chopped
1 red or green bell pepper, sliced
½ bunch cilantro, leaves finely chopped
½ teaspoon ground cumin
¼ teaspoon ground cinnamon
Pinch ground cardamom
Pinch ground cloves
Pinch nutmeg, freshly ground

Rinse the fish inside and out and pat dry with paper towels. Cut 3 diagonal slits on each side of the fish for even cooking. The deep angled pockets also allow you to thoroughly season the flesh and skin. Sprinkle the outside of the fish with salt and rub with the lemon quarters to remove the fishy odor and any discoloration.

In a large mixing bowl, combine the stuffing ingredients. Mix well, then fill the cavity of the fish with the stuffing. Stitch the cavity shut with butcher's twine, if available. Wrap up the fish with large fig leaves or foil.

Combine all of the sauce ingredients in a jar. Close the lid and shake it to mix well. Set aside.

Prepare a gas or charcoal grill. Grill the wrapped fish over medium heat for 8 to 10 minutes per inch (2.5 cm) of thickness. Check for doneness inside the slit, at the thickest part of the fish. The flesh should be firm and opaque and separate easily from the bone.

Transfer to a serving dish. Unfold the leaves or foil and top the fish with the sauce. Garnish with lemon wedges and serve.

*Continued on next page*

¼ teaspoon freshly ground
 black pepper
¼ cup (60 ml) freshly squeezed
 lemon juice
½ cup (120 ml) extra-virgin olive oil

**SPICY SAUCE**
1 tablespoon red pepper paste
 (p. 200)
1 lemon freshly squeezed
3–4 garlic cloves, crushed
¼ cup (60 ml) extra-virgin olive oil

# MAIN
# DISHES

# MAIN DISHES

## *Tabkha*

The morning ritual for many mothers in Lebanon begins with a big pot of Arabic coffee, and perhaps a short *sobhiyeh*—a morning gathering with neighbors and friends. The children have already left early for school, so it's a time for reflection. What will the daily dish (*tabkha*) be for the family today? The daily *tabkha* is taken seriously by all members of the household. Children come home asking what's for dinner. Families cherish daily meals around the table together, putting the stresses of the day behind them.

The cooking most often starts by chopping onions and garlic to fry in oil. Walking through the streets of Beirut in the early morning, you can count on the distinctive aroma of fried onions and garlic wafting through the streets. If you are missing an ingredient, you can quickly go to a small nearby market (*dekken*) to pick up a few pieces of produce needed to make a recipe. Moms who work during the day prepare food at night for the next day. Meals are planned, organized, and certainly not taken lightly.

As a young mother with three children, the most important task I set out for myself on a daily basis was to provide a wholesome cooked meal for my family. When this was done, I could organize the rest of the day accordingly. Unlike others I knew, I would never plan ahead. I would make use of available ingredients on hand and choose a dish to make based on my own cravings or the ones any member of the family might express during a particular week. If the pantry is well stocked and there are meats in the freezer, the task is doable.

Most meals require fresh vegetables, and I am lucky and privileged to have a grocer who can deliver to me very quickly, as his produce shop is nearby. We have a special relationship, often discussing food stories on the phone. He always sends me the first choice of produce. For organic produce, I visit the weekly farmers' market to pick seasonal fruit and vegetables. According to what is available, I decide what to cook.

Lebanese home-cooked dishes are most often stews, with or without meats. Ingredients are cooked slowly on the stovetop and served with bulgur or rice, and a salad on the side. Many households have a weekly repertoire that they follow throughout the year, making use of the availability of seasonal products.

One of my favorite *tabkha* is *kousa mehshi*—Stuffed Zucchini (p. 170). My eldest daughter, Maria, complained as a young girl that she was tired of eating this dish. Years later, when she traveled abroad to study, I asked her what dish I should prepare to make her happy when she came home to visit. She answered, "*Kousa mehshi*—yum, yum, yum!" an expression she used as a child. The foods you eat at home as a child build memories for a lifetime. Family recipes survive across generations and help protect our culinary heritage and our identity as a people.

**Left:** Candid shot of a young woman on the streets of Beirut during *Thawra*, the Lebanese revolution.

# Mixed Beans and Grains

## *Makhlouta*

*Makhlouta* can be eaten as a hearty soup appetizer, but is often *the* main dish, especially on cold winter days. It is filling, wholesome, and versatile: gather and use whatever beans or grains you have in your pantry. I love the rustic flavors and traditions of the countryside. I collect old spoons to remind myself of days when all you needed to feed yourself was a wooden spoon, personalized and easily accessible for all your meals. Beans and grains are an important staple in the Lebanese diet, especially for those living in the mountains, as they are full of protein to nourish and strengthen the body. Those who are vegans or vegetarians will appreciate this thick porridge-like dish. You will need to soak your beans overnight.

½ cup (100 g) dried chickpeas

½ cup (100 g) dried red kidney beans

½ cup (100 g) dried white kidney beans

⅓ cup (60g) brown lentils

⅓ cup (50 g) coarse bulgur

3 tablespoons extra-virgin olive oil, plus extra to serve

2 large onions, sliced

1 teaspoon ground cumin

1 teaspoon salt

Pinch freshly ground black pepper

2 lemon wedges, to serve

Soak the chickpeas and red and white kidney beans separately in plenty of water overnight. The next day, rinse well and drain, discarding any impurities.

Place the drained chickpeas and beans into a large pot and cover with plenty of water. Bring to a boil, then lower the heat and simmer for about 90 minutes until tender but still firm, topping up the water as needed (you can do this in a pressure cooker, if you have one, to save time). Add the lentils and bulgur and continue to simmer for 15 minutes, until your grains and legumes are tender (the timing will vary depending on how old your dried beans are).

In a frying pan, heat the olive oil over medium heat and sauté the onions for about 5 minutes to soften. Add the cumin and continue to cook for another minute or two. Add the onions to the hot bean and grain mixture.

Simmer the bean mixture for an additional 15 to 20 minutes, until thick and porridge-like. Season with salt and pepper to taste. Serve hot with a splash of olive oil and lemon wedges on the side.

# Fisherman's Catch

## *Sayadiyeh*

*Sayadiyeh* translates to "the fisherman's catch." It is a dish of baked fish with flavorful rice that is topped with caramelized onions, nuts, and a lemony sauce. Chef Habib Hadid is my go-to reference for local seafood dishes. His pioneering restaurant Le Phenicien has been introducing locals and international visitors to a wealth of local seafood dishes since 1988. We have shared countless food memories both in his restaurant in Beirut and the one overlooking the sea in the coastal city of Tyre, one of the earliest Phoenician cities (hence the name of his restaurant). Hospitality and generosity are key ingredients to becoming a successful restaurateur, and he has both qualities. On every occasion I go, sometimes unannounced, I am treated to an unbelievable seafood spread with countless plates of food.

2¼ lb (1 kg) whole white fish, such as sea bass, halibut, red snapper, or cod, scaled and gutted (or use boneless fillets)

1 tablespoon salt

1 lemon, cut into thin wedges, plus extra to serve

2 cups (400 g) long-grain white rice

Pinch ground cinnamon

½ teaspoon ground cumin

1 teaspoon ground caraway

¼ teaspoon ground allspice

¼ teaspoon ground white pepper

1 cup (140 g) pine nuts

¼ cup (30 g) slivered or halved almonds

4¼ cups (1 liter) fish stock (preferably homemade, see below)

3 large onions, sliced

Extra-virgin olive oil

*Continued on next page*

To make the fish stock, heat the olive oil in a large pot over medium heat and sauté the onion until soft. Add the fish heads and bones and 8 cups (2 liters) of water. Bring to a boil, skimming any foam from the surface. Add the spices, reduce the heat, and simmer for 1 hour. Strain the broth through a fine sieve over a large pot. Set aside.

Preheat the oven to 400°F (200°C). Line a baking pan with aluminum foil. Place the fish on the pan, brush it all over with 2 tablespoons of oil, sprinkle with salt, and place the lemon wedges inside and on top of the fish. Wrap the fish in the foil and bake until the flesh flakes easily with a fork, 20 to 25 minutes for a whole fish, or 15 to 20 minutes for fillets. Set aside until cool enough to handle, then separate the flesh from the bones and skin. Place the flesh in a saucepan with a few tablespoons of the stock so it doesn't dry out, cover, and set aside. Discard the skin and bones.

Heat 2 tablespoons of olive oil in a pot over low heat. Add the rice and spices and stir for 1 minute until the rice is coated. Add the 4¼ cups (1 liter) of the fish stock, bring to a boil, then reduce the heat to very low, cover, and simmer for 10 minutes. Remove from the heat and let the rice stand with the lid on.

In a nonstick frying pan, fry the pine nuts and almonds separately, each in 1 tablespoon of olive oil. Set aside. Add 2 tablespoons of olive oil to the pan and fry the onions over medium heat, stirring occasionally, for about 15 minutes, until golden brown and caramelized. Spread the fried onions out on a plate lined with paper towels. Leave to cool.

## SAUCE

¼ cup (60 g) clarified butter
  or butter
¼ cup (30 g) all-purpose flour
3 cups (700 ml) cold fish stock
  (preferably homemade,
  see below)
Freshly squeezed lemon juice,
  to taste

## FISH STOCK

1 tablespoon extra-virgin olive oil
1 large onion, coarsely chopped
1 lb (450 g) fish heads and bones
1 cinnamon stick
3–4 allspice berries
1 bay leaf
1 teaspoon coarse sea salt
3–4 black peppercorns

To make the sauce, melt the clarified butter in a sauté pan over medium heat. Add the flour and cook, whisking constantly, until dark in color, about 2 minutes. Whisk in 3 cups (700 ml) of the cold fish stock, one ladle at a time, whisking until smooth between each addition. Turn down the heat and simmer until it thickens, 3 to 5 minutes. Add the lemon juice and continue to simmer, stirring constantly, for 30 minutes for the flavors to come together.

Fluff the rice and mount it onto a large platter. Arrange the fish on top, then sprinkle with the onions, then the nuts. Drizzle with the sauce, and serve with lemon wedges.

# Eggplants Stuffed with Meat

## *Sheikh el Mehshi*

*Sheikh* means "the head of" usually a tribe, family, or village. This dish of eggplant stuffed with spiced meat in a rich tomato sauce will certainly not go unnoticed on your table. It is best to use small eggplants in perfect condition and of similar size. I was once invited to Edinburgh by Chef Ben Reade and his partner, Sashana Souza Zanella, to be a guest chef in their restaurant, Food Studio. The menu showcased dishes from Lebanon, including a twist on *sheikh el mehshi*. Ben's excellent kitchen staff scurried around, asking me "chef this, chef that." I suddenly felt overwhelmed and said, "from now on, you will call me Auntie Barbara." And that is exactly what they did. The kitchen ambiance changed, our guests were satisfied, and Ben introduced his guest chef, "Auntie Barbara," to his customers.

2¼ lb (1 kg) small eggplants

Vegetable oil, for deep-frying

2 tablespoons extra-virgin olive oil

3–4 tablespoons pine nuts

1 tablespoon butter

1 large onion, finely chopped

8 oz (250 g) ground beef or lamb with 15% fat

¼ teaspoon ground cinnamon

½ teaspoon ground allspice

1 teaspoon salt, plus extra to taste

¼ teaspoon freshly ground black pepper

**TOMATO SAUCE**

4 tomatoes, finely chopped

1 tablespoon tomato paste diluted with 1 cup (240 ml) water

1 tablespoon pomegranate molasses (optional)

½ teaspoon salt

¼ teaspoon freshly ground black pepper

Slit each eggplant down the middle, three-quarters of the way through. Pat dry. Pour vegetable oil into a large pot or deep-fryer to a depth of 2 in (5 cm). Heat until the oil reaches a temperature of 350°F (180°C), or until small bubbles gather around a piece of bread dropped into the oil. Working in batches, fry the eggplants for 10 to 15 minutes, turning halfway through, until they soften and change color. Transfer to a colander or a plate lined with paper towels to drain excess oil. Set aside.

In a large nonstick frying pan, fry the pine nuts in 1 tablespoon of the olive oil until golden, watching carefully so they don't burn. Transfer to a plate lined with paper towels and set aside. In the same pan, sauté the onion in the remaining 1 tablespoon of olive oil and the butter until golden. Add the ground beef, spices, salt, and pepper. Sauté for 10 to 15 minutes until well browned. Add half of the pine nuts and set aside.

Make the tomato sauce: In a sauté pan or pot, combine the tomatoes, diluted tomato paste, and pomegranate molasses (if using), and bring to a boil. Lower the heat and simmer for 20 minutes, stirring occasionally. Remove from the heat and use a handheld immersion blender or blender to purée until smooth. Mix in the salt and pepper.

Preheat the oven to 350°F (180°C) and arrange the eggplants in a large baking dish, slit side up. Use a fork to widen the openings and loosen the flesh inside. Season with salt. Add half the tomato sauce to the ground meat mixture and stir well. Use this to generously stuff the eggplants, mixing with a fork so the meat and eggplant flesh are combined. Ladle the rest of the tomato sauce over the eggplants so they are well covered. Bake for 30 minutes, until the eggplants are cooked. Garnish with the remaining pine nuts and serve with rice or Vermicelli Rice (p. 177).

# Lamb in Yogurt

## *Laban Ummo*

In this dish, lamb is cooked in a rich yogurt sauce. *Laban ummo* literally means "its mother's milk," since, in the past, the sauce was made from sheep or goat milk, particularly in mountains of Lebanon, where herding is common. Rice with yogurt is a popular remedy for an upset stomach in Lebanon and this rich stew, typically served with rice, is a comforting homemade meal to build strength or lift one's spirit.

1 lb (450 g) boneless lamb shanks, cut into chunks

1 large onion, quartered

1 bay leaf

1 cinnamon sticks

3 cloves

2 cardamom pods

2–3 allspice berries

1 tablespoon coarse sea salt

### YOGURT SAUCE

4½ cups (1 kg) plain yogurt

1 large egg, whisked

1 teaspoon salt

1½ tablespoon cornstarch mixed with ¼ cup (60 ml) water

An hour before you cook the yogurt sauce, it is best to bring out the yogurt from the refrigerator and let it stand at room temperature.

Place the lamb in a large pot and cover with water. Bring to a boil, skimming the foam from the surface. Add the onion, bay leaf, cinnamon stick, cloves, cardamom, allspice, and salt. Reduce the heat, cover, and simmer for 1½ to 2 hours, until the meat is very tender (you can do this in a pressure cooker, if you have one, to save time). Strain the broth through a fine sieve, and set the meat and broth aside.

Make the sauce: Put the yogurt in large pot and set over medium heat. Whisk in the egg and salt and bring to a boil, whisking constantly in the same direction to avoid curdling. As soon as the yogurt starts to boil, lower the heat to low and add the diluted cornstarch and 1 cup (240 ml) of the warm lamb broth. Simmer, stirring constantly, for 15 minutes, until the sauce thickens. Add the meat and simmer for an additional 10 minutes.

Serve with rice or Vermicelli Rice (p. 177).

# Roasted Green Wheat with Chicken

*Freekeh*

Chefs all over the world are raving about freekeh, an age-old specialty of Lebanon and neighboring countries—Syria, Jordan, Egypt, and Palestine. Freekeh is a roasted, parched green wheat grain with a chewy texture and a smoky, nutty flavor. The word freekeh comes from the Arabic word *al-freek* meaning "what is rubbed" referring to the traditional process of making freekeh, which involves rubbing the wheat grains with one's hands to free them of their shell. I visited several villages at the border in South Lebanon to witness the process. At the end of the day, I was invited to dine with freekeh producers and their families; we sat on the floor on makeshift sofas to share a lavish meal centered around this local specialty.

Freekeh can be served as an accompaniment to meat, poultry, and seafood dishes, as a hearty substitute for rice in stuffed vegetable dishes, and to give texture to soups or salads. It can even be used to make delicious breads. Freekeh has also become popular among vegetarians for its hearty texture and smoked flavor. Here, it is served with chicken and fried nuts. Before you start, freekeh should be soaked in water for at least an hour.

2 cups (400 g) whole freekeh
½ cup (70 g) pine nuts
½ cup (60 g) slivered almonds
½ cup (60 g) shelled pistachios
1 tablespoon butter
1 large onion, finely chopped
1 teaspoon ground allspice
½ teaspoon ground cinnamon
⅓ teaspoon ground nutmeg
¼ teaspoon ground black pepper
1 teaspoon salt
Extra-virgin olive oil

## CHICKEN AND BROTH

5 lb (2.25 kg) free-range chicken
1 large onion, quartered
1 carrot, sliced
1–2 bay leaves
1 cinnamon stick
2–3 allspice berries
1 tablespoon coarse sea salt

Spread the freekeh out on a tray and pick through it to remove any impurities. Rinse under cold running water, drain, and soak in plenty of fresh water overnight, or for at least 1 hour. Drain well.

Prepare the chicken and broth: Place the chicken in a large stockpot and cover with water. Bring to a boil, skimming any foam from the surface. Add the remaining broth ingredients. Reduce the heat and simmer until the chicken is cooked, 45 minutes. Reserving the broth, transfer the chicken to a chopping board, remove the bones, and cut it into bite-size pieces. Return the chicken to the pot with a few tablespoons of broth so it doesn't dry out. Strain the remaining broth and measure out 4¼ cups (1 liter). Set aside.

In a small frying pan, heat 1 tablespoon of olive oil and fry the pine nuts, almonds, and pistachios separately until golden, adding more oil as needed. Transfer to a plate lined with paper towels to drain excess oil.

In a large pot, heat the butter and 1 tablespoon of olive oil and sauté the onion until golden. Add the drained freekeh and spices and mix until the grains are coated. Warm the reserved chicken broth. Mix 1 ladleful of hot chicken broth into the freekeh, stirring over medium-low heat until it is absorbed. Repeat until the freekeh is tender, but still has some bite. This will take 45 minutes to an hour in total (you may not need all of the broth).

Just before serving, gently reheat the chicken. Transfer the freekeh to a large serving dish, top with the chicken, and garnish with fried nuts.

# Pearl Couscous

## *Moghrabiyeh*

*Moghrabiyeh* is the name of both this pilaf-like dish, and its central ingredient, a durum wheat semolina-based couscous similar to the North African staple—hence the name, which translates to "of the Maghreb." Lebanese couscous resembles North African couscous in texture and shape, but is much larger. The grains are bought dry from local grocers, or fresh or frozen from specialty shops around Lebanon. *Moghrabiyeh* is often made for feasts, topped with pearl onions and a thick sauce, and served alongside lamb shank or chicken. In the old souk of Tripoli in North Lebanon, you can buy a delicious vegetarian sandwich stuffed with a version of *moghrabiyeh*—a feast of carbs that will definitely fill your belly. The simple recipe below is my favorite way to eat *moghrabiyeh*. You will need to soak the dried chickpeas overnight, so plan accordingly.

1 cup (200 g) dried chickpeas

Pinch baking soda (if your chickpeas are old)

⅔ cup (250 g) dried *moghrabiyeh* (pearl or giant couscous)

¼ cup (60 ml) extra-virgin olive oil

1 tablespoon butter or clarified butter

8 oz (250 g) peeled pearl onions, or 2 large onions, sliced

1 tablespoon ground caraway

1 teaspoon ground cinnamon

1–2 bay leaves

1 teaspoon ground cumin

1 teaspoon Lebanese 7-spice (*baharat*) or ground allspice

¼ teaspoon freshly ground black pepper

1 teaspoon salt

Soak the chickpeas in water overnight with the baking soda, if using. Rinse and drain the chickpeas, and transfer them to a pot with plenty of fresh water. Bring to a boil, then reduce the heat and simmer until the chickpeas are tender, but still hold their shape, 30 to 45 minutes depending on how fresh your dried chickpeas are. Test by squeezing a chickpea between your fingers; it should break apart. Drain and set aside.

Cook the *moghrabiyeh* in a large pot of salted boiling water until al-dente, 10 to 15 minutes, or according to your package instructions. Drain, reserving the cooking water.

Heat the olive oil and butter a large pot and fry the onion until golden. Add the chickpeas and spices and mix until the chickpeas are coated. Add the cooked pearl couscous and 1 cup (240 ml) of the reserved cooking water. Mix gently so you don't crush them and cook until heated through. If the mixture seems dry, mix in a little more of the cooking water.

Serve warm with salad on the side, or in a sandwich with Arabic bread (p. 28) and pickles.

# Lentils and Rice

## *Mujaddara*

This dish of lentils, rice, spices, and caramelized onions is the Massaad family's Friday dinner. *Mujaddara* is a favorite main dish during Lent, when many Christians abstain from eating meat, but many Lebanese families continue this ritual on Fridays throughout the year. Local restaurants also often follow this trend. Once cooked, *mujaddara* is divided among individual shallow serving dishes, ready for the family meal. It's very convenient, since it is best eaten at room temperature.

There are numerous regional variations of this dish. In the north of Lebanon, it is made with red beans and bulgur; while in the south, the dish takes on a lighter color as it is made with split yellow lentils and rice. Either way, *mujaddara* is always served with salad, preferably made of cabbage, or sliced raw onions, radishes, and mint. In our house, we served *mujaddara* with pickled cabbage (colored pink from the addition of beets) made by our dear late friend and small-scale food producer Amal Harb.

½ cup (100 g) short-grain white rice

2 cups (400 g) brown lentils

3 large onions, 1 finely chopped, and 2 thinly sliced

½ teaspoon ground allspice

½ teaspoon ground cumin

1 teaspoon salt

½ teaspoon freshly ground black pepper

Extra-virgin olive oil

Rinse the rice, then soak in water for at least 30 minutes. Drain.

Spread the lentils out on a tray and pick through them to remove any small stones or impurities. Rinse under cold running water and drain well.

Heat 1 tablespoon of olive oil in a large pot and sauté the chopped onion until translucent, but not browned. Add the lentils and 4¼ cups (1 liter) of water, or enough to cover them. Bring to a boil, then lower the heat and simmer until tender, about 20 minutes.

Pass the lentils through a food mill using the finest setting, discarding the skins, or use a handheld immersion blender or food processor to blend until smooth. Return the lentils to the pot, add the drained rice, and place over medium heat, stirring constantly to ensure the mixture doesn't stick to the bottom of the pot (you can add a splash of water if needed). Cook, stirring, for 20 to 25 minutes, until the rice is cooked. Add the allspice, cumin, salt, and pepper.

Heat 2 tablespoons of olive oil in a large frying pan over medium heat and fry the sliced onions, stirring occasionally, until golden and caramelized, about 15 minutes. Spread the onions out on a plate lined with paper towels to cool.

Spoon the lentil mixture onto individual shallow serving dishes and set aside to cool to room temperature. Top with the caramelized onions and serve with plenty of Arabic bread (p. 28) and pickles or a fresh salad dressed with lemon juice, olive oil, garlic, and salt.

# Jute Mallow Stew

## Mloukhiyeh

Mloukhiyeh translates to jute mallow, a leafy green commonly found in the Middle East and North Africa. The name may be derived from the Arabic word *molokiya*, meaning royalty—certainly not an understatement! The majestic dark green leaves grow on tall stems and are the prized main ingredient in a dish that carries the same name. Preparing the leaves is a joyful culinary ritual for me; I love to make and eat this dish, surrounded by family and friends. Every year, I buy huge quantities of leaves, wash them, and put them out to dry in the garden overnight. The next day, I chop them finely and freeze them to use throughout the year. In the dish, the leaves, chopped or left whole, are cooked in broth seasoned with fried garlic and cilantro. The hot stew is served with pieces of meat, chicken, or both over cooked rice, with toasted Arabic bread, and onions pickled in vinegar alongside. At our house, we always make *mloukhiyeh* with chicken.

5 lb (2.25 kg) free-range whole chicken or chicken pieces

1 large onion, quartered

1–2 bay leaves

1 cinnamon stick

2–3 allspice berries

1 tablespoon coarse sea salt

2 large bunches fresh *mloukhiyeh* (jute mallow) or 5 cups (150 g) soaked dried leaves, rinsed and drained, stalks removed, leaves left whole or shredded; or use two 14 oz (400 g) packages of frozen *mloukhiyeh*, thawed

4 tablespoons extra-virgin olive oil

4 garlic cloves, minced

1 bunch cilantro, finely chopped

**TO SERVE**

1 large onion, finely chopped

1 cup (240 ml) apple cider vinegar

2 Arabic bread (p. 28), toasted

Vermicelli Rice (p. 177), to serve

Prepare the chicken and broth: Place the chicken in a large stockpot and cover with 4 quarts (4 liters) of water. Bring to a boil, skimming any foam from the surface. Add the onion, bay leaves, cinnamon sticks, allspice, and salt. Reduce the heat and simmer until the chicken is cooked, 45 minutes. Reserving the broth, transfer the chicken to a chopping board, pick the meat off the bones, and cut it into bite-size pieces. Place the chicken in a small pot with 1 cup (240 ml) of the broth so it doesn't dry out. Strain the remaining broth through a fine sieve and return it to the stockpot.

Bring the broth to a boil, add the *mloukhiyeh* leaves, lower the heat, and simmer until wilted and tender, 15 to 20 minutes for fresh or rehydrated leaves, or 10 minutes for frozen.

Meanwhile, heat the oil in a small frying pan and sauté the garlic until golden. Mix in the cilantro, lower the heat, and cook just until the leaves wilt. Stir this mixture into the simmering *mloukhiyeh*.

In a small bowl, mix the chopped onion with the vinegar and set aside.

Toast the bread under your broiler until brown and crisp, and break into bite-size pieces. Place in a bowl.

Place the Vermicelli Rice in a serving bowl. Reheat the chicken and transfer to a serving dish.

This dish is best assembled at the table, so serve all of the components separately. To eat, spread a handful of toasted bread in the base of your bowl. Top with a serving of rice, followed by some chicken, then a ladleful of *mloukhiyeh*. Top with the vinegared onions.

# Stuffed Zucchini

## *Kousa Mehshi*

In this popular dish, vegetables are stuffed with rice and meat, layered in a pot, and cooked in a tomato sauce, for an impressive one-pot dinner that also makes excellent leftovers. The main ingredient in this recipe is zucchini, but that does not mean that one cannot add small eggplants, bell peppers, and a few rolled grape leaves to the pot. There are many stuffed vegetable dishes. The process starts at the market, where one must go early and nudge through crowds of like-minded customers to pick the best zucchini money can buy. They should be medium in size—each about 6 in (15 cm) long—and shaped alike to ensure even cooking. Coring the vegetables with a sharp-edged vegetable corer takes practice. The aim is to hollow it out, leaving a very thin wall to hold a good amount of stuffing. I've had my share of broken vegetables, but this never stopped me from stuffing them to cook; they just didn't look perfect. Never throw out the insides; mixed with some herbs, they make for a delicious omelet.

3 lb 5 oz (1.5 kg) small, evenly sized
  zucchini, tops cut off, cored

1 lb (450 g) baby eggplants,
  tops cut off, cored

2 bell peppers, tops cut off,
  hollowed (optional)

Plain yogurt or labneh (see p. 94),
  to serve (optional)

**STUFFING**

1 cup (200 g) short-grain white rice

8 oz (250 g) ground beef or lamb
  with 25% fat for the best flavor

1 small tomato, finely chopped

1 teaspoon salt

½ teaspoon ground allspice

½ teaspoon ground cinnamon

½ teaspoon ground cumin

1 teaspoon red pepper paste (p. 200)

*Continued on next page*

To make the stuffing, soak the rice in cold water for at least 30 minutes, and drain well. In a mixing bowl, combine the rice with the remaining stuffing ingredients and mix thoroughly with your hands. Stuff the vegetables two-thirds full with the mixture, leaving enough space for the rice to expand during cooking. Leave the bell peppers for last to use up the rest of the stuffing.

Make the sauce: In an 8 quart (8 liter) pot, heat the olive oil and sauté the onion until soft. Add the garlic, spices, parsley, mint, and salt and cook for 2 minutes. Add the chopped tomatoes and diluted tomato paste and simmer for a couple of minutes until the flavors come together. Mix in the stock. Layer the stuffed vegetables on their sides in the pot as close together as you can. Weigh the top of the vegetables down with a heat-safe plate to keep them immersed in the sauce (you can add a little more stock if needed, but not too much), then cover the pot. Bring to a boil, then lower the heat and simmer for 1 hour, until the vegetables are tender and the rice is cooked.

Serve hot with yogurt or labneh on the side.

## TOMATO SAUCE

3 tablespoons extra-virgin olive oil

1 onion, finely chopped

3 garlic cloves, minced

½ teaspoon ground allspice

½ teaspoon ground cinnamon

½ teaspoon ground cumin

½ teaspoon freshly ground
   black pepper

2 tablespoons finely chopped
   flat-leaf parsley

1 tablespoon finely chopped
   mint leaves

1 teaspoon salt

4 ripe tomatoes, finely chopped

1 tablespoon tomato paste diluted
   with 1 cup (240 ml) water

6 cups (1.5 liters) chicken, beef, or
   vegetable stock or water

# Stuffed Grape Leaves with Meat

## *Warak Enab wa Lahmeh*

This hearty main dish takes several hours to prepare, but don't let that discourage you from making it—the results are well worth it. You will see them disappear in minutes (like with all labor-intensive dishes, this can be quite frustrating sometimes). There are many different variations of this dish, from country to country and even from household to household. I learned how to make it during my training sessions in a famous Lebanese restaurant called Abdel Wahab, and again from a Lebanese mama. The taste is very different from the vegetarian version (p. 58) that is often served as a mezze.

In Lebanon, we make *warak enab* in late spring to early summer, when fresh grape vine leaves are healthy, tender, unblemished, and in abundance. The leaves should be about the size of the palm of your hand and free of pesticides. Very young leaves can tear easily; older ones can be tough and chewy. Those who live in the mountains of Lebanon often make use of the *arishe* (vines) overhanging their balcony or terrace. Otherwise, fresh leaves are sold in farmers' markets, but you can also find them jarred in brine or vacuum-packed.

70 to 80 young grape vine leaves, stems removed, or a 16 oz (450 g) jar of grape vine leaves

1 lb (450 g) boneless lamb shank, cut into chunks

1 tablespoon salt

1 tablespoon vegetable oil

2–3 lamb bones, cleaned (optional)

A few lettuce leaves (optional)

Juice of 1–2 lemons

Plain yogurt, to serve (optional)

*Continued on next page*

If you are using fresh grape leaves, blanch them in salted boiling water for 1 minute, then immediately transfer them to cold water to stop the cooking process. If using jarred grape leaves, rinse thoroughly. Drain and set aside.

Mix all the stuffing ingredients in a large bowl.

Flatten a leaf on the table in front of you, rough side up, with the stem end closest to you. Place 1 full teaspoon of stuffing in a horizontal line across the middle. Fold the sides inwards and roll up like a cigar. Make sure the stuffing is completely covered and the leaf is tightly and securely wrapped, but not so tight that the rice doesn't have room to expand. This is where the expertise lies. Repeat to finish all the stuffing.

Season the lamb with salt. In a large stockpot, heat the vegetable oil and sear the lamb and the bones over high heat for 2 to 3 minutes on each side until browned. Arrange the lamb and bones neatly on the bottom of the pot. Layer the stuffed grape leaves over the meat and bones, around the edge of the pot, seam side down, and then layer the rest across the middle. Repeat until you have even layers. Cover the grape leaves with lettuce leaves to avoid oxidation. Add the lemon juice and enough water to cover the leaves by about 1 in (2.5 cm). Weigh the top of down with a heat-safe plate to keep the rolls immersed in the liquid, then cover the pot.

## STUFFING

1 lb (450 g) finely ground beef or
   lamb with 25% fat for the
   best flavor
1¼ cups (250 g) short-grain white
   rice, soaked in cold water for
   30 minutes
¼ cup (60 ml) extra-virgin olive oil
½ teaspoon ground cinnamon
¼ teaspoon freshly ground
   black pepper
1 teaspoon ground allspice
1 tablespoon salt

Bring to a boil, then lower the heat and simmer for 1 to 1½ hours, until the rice is cooked. Uncover and leave to cool in the pot for 10 minutes.

Place a large serving dish face down over the pot. Holding the dish firmly in place, flip the pot over and let the contents drop into the serving dish. Serve warm with a side of yogurt.

# Meatball Stew
## *Dawoud Basha*

According to legend, this dish was named for a high ranking official during Ottoman rule in Lebanon. *Dawoud* is Arabic for David and *basha* is an Ottoman class title equivalent to lord (the actual word is *pasha* but the letter "P" does not exist in Arabic). This title was given to high-ranking personnel, such as army generals or governors. In this dish, hearty meatballs are cooked in a rich tomato sauce and served with rice or bulgur. I serve this dish with a typical Lebanese rice pilaf that is made daily in most Lebanese households—rice with broken vermicelli. It is a meal fit for a lord or lady.

1 lb (450 g) ground beef or lamb
  with 25% fat for the best flavor
1 medium onion, finely chopped
¼ teaspoon ground allspice
Pinch ground cinnamon
½ teaspoon salt
Pinch freshly ground black pepper
1 tablespoon butter
1 tablespoon vegetable oil
Vermicelli Rice (see facing page),
  to serve

**TOMATO SAUCE**
1 large onion, sliced
Pinch ground clove
Pinch nutmeg, freshly ground
¼ teaspoon ground cinnamon
4–6 ripe tomatoes, finely chopped
1 tablespoon tomato paste diluted
  with 1 cup (240 ml) water
4¼ cups (1 liter) vegetable or
  beef stock

In a large mixing bowl, combine the meat with onion, spices, salt, and pepper. Form into 1 in (3 cm) meatballs.

In a large sauté pan, heat the butter and oil over medium heat and brown the meatballs on all sides (you can also bake them in the oven for 30 minutes at 350°F (180°C), turning them half way through). Transfer to a plate.

In the same pan, make the sauce: Add the onion and spices and sauté with the drippings until the onions are translucent. Add the chopped tomatoes, diluted tomato paste, and stock. Bring to a boil, then reduce the heat and simmer for 15 to 20 minutes until the sauce thickens. Add the meatballs and continue to simmer for 15 minutes until cooked through.

Serve the meatball stew with Vermicelli Rice.

# Vermicelli Rice  SERVES 4 TO 6
*Shariyeh*

2 cups (400 g) short-grain white rice
2 tablespoons butter
1 tablespoon extra-virgin olive oil
6 tablespoons broken vermicelli
   (made from durum wheat)
3 cups (700 ml) water
1 tablespoon salt

Rinse the rice in several changes of cold water and drain well. In a pot, melt the butter and olive oil over medium heat and cook the vermicelli, stirring constantly, until golden brown. Stir in the rice and continue to cook, stirring, for a minute or two until well coated. Add the water and salt, then bring to a boil, cover, lower the heat, and simmer for 15 minutes until the rice is cooked. Turn off the heat and let stand for 5 minutes before fluffing with a fork.

# Meat Dumplings in Yogurt

## *Shish Barak*

If you are not familiar with *shish barak*, you can compare it to Italian tortellini or Armenian *manti*. Small dumplings are filled with a mixture of ground beef, onion, and parsley, baked or fried, and served in a warm yogurt sauce flavored with garlic, cilantro, and olive oil, with rice alongside. You can make double the quantity of dumplings to store in the freezer for a last-minute meal for your family. When my youngest daughter, Sarah, returned from a year of studying in the UK, she asked me to fill our freezer with *shish barak*. The dish always reminds me that home cooking always tastes best.

### FILLING

1 small onion, very finely chopped

¼ teaspoon ground allspice

½ teaspoon salt

Pinch freshly ground black pepper

8 oz (240 g) ground beef with
    20% fat

½ small bunch flat-leaf parsley,
    finely chopped by hand

### DOUGH

2½ cups (300 g) all-purpose flour,
    plus extra for dusting

1 tablespoon extra-virgin olive oil
    or butter

1½ cups (350 ml) water

½ teaspoon salt

*Continued on next page*

Make the filling: In a mixing bowl, combine the chopped onion, allspice, salt, and pepper. Place the meat on a clean work surface and mix in the chopped parsley and onion mixture. Knead until you have a homogeneous dough-like consistency. Refrigerate while you make the dough.

In a food processor, stand mixer, or mixing bowl, combine all of the dough ingredients until they come together. Knead just until you have a pliable dough. Let rest for 30 minutes. Lightly dust your work surface with flour and roll the dough out as thinly as you can manage—ideally 2 to 3 mm thick. Use a 2 in (5 cm) round cutter or glass to cut out circles, rerolling until you have used up all of the dough. Place ¼ teaspoon of stuffing in the center of each dough round. Fold in half and seal the edges together over the stuffing to form a semicircle, then bring the corners together and pinch them to seal (somewhat like forming tortellini). Dust a large baking tray with flour and arrange the finished dumplings on it. (If you are freezing, cover with plastic wrap and place the tray in the freezer for a couple of hours, then pack them into storage bags and return to the freezer. You can bake or deep-fry them from frozen.)

To bake the dumplings: Preheat the oven to 350°F (180°C) . Bake the *shish barak* for 10 to 15 minutes until crisp. Alternatively, you can deep-fry them: Pour vegetable oil into a large pot or deep-fryer to a depth of 2 in (5 cm). Heat until the oil reaches a temperature of 350°F (180°C), or until small bubbles gather around a small piece of bread dropped into the oil. Working in batches, fry the *shish barak* for 2 minutes, until cooked and golden. Transfer to a metal colander or a plate lined with paper towels to drain excess oil. Set aside.

## YOGURT SAUCE

4½ cups (1 kg) plain yogurt,
  at room temperature
1 large egg, whisked
1 teaspoon salt
1½ tablespoon cornstarch mixed
  with ¼ cup (60 ml) water
2 tablespoons extra-virgin olive oil
2–3 garlic cloves, minced
1 bunch mint or cilantro, leaves
  finely chopped, or 1 tablespoon
  dried mint

Vegetable oil, for deep-frying
  (optional)

Make the sauce: Put the yogurt in a saucepan and set over medium heat. Add the egg and salt and bring to a boil, whisking constantly in the same direction to prevent the yogurt from curdling (egg helps with this). As soon as the yogurt starts to bubble, lower the heat to a gentle simmer and whisk in the cornstarch water. Simmer, whisking constantly, for 10 minutes, until the sauce has thickened.

Meanwhile, heat the oil in a small frying pan over medium heat and sauté the garlic just until golden. Mix in the mint or cilantro, lower the heat, and cook just until the leaves have just wilted, but are still green. Mix into the simmering yogurt.

Carefully drop the dumplings into the yogurt sauce, and gently heat through. Serve hot with rice or Vermicelli Rice (p. 177).

# Spicy Fish

## *Samkeh Harra*

This dish is a specialty of the coastal city of Tripoli, the second largest city in Lebanon. As a child, I never really liked eating fish or seafood. Of course, with time, everything changed for the better and *samkeh harra* is now one of my favorite dishes. The stuffing is full of flavor, texture, and vibrant color. I often compare cooking with art, as it is a form of expression for every cook. Prepare this recipe for your next occasion or gathering—it will make an everlasting impression on your guests. It can be served a variety of ways.

4½ lb (2 kg) whole white fish, such
   as sea bass, sea bream, or cod,
   scaled and gutted
1 teaspoon salt
½ cup (70 g) pine nuts
1 whole garlic bulb, cloves peeled
1 teaspoon ground coriander
1 bunch cilantro, finely chopped
1 onion, finely chopped
1 green chile pepper,
   finely chopped
1 tomato, diced
½ cup (120 ml) extra-virgin olive oil,
   plus extra for greasing
Juice of 2 lemons
1 teaspoon ground cumin
¼ teaspoon freshly ground
   black pepper
½ teaspoon Aleppo pepper
   or cayenne

**TO SERVE (OPTIONAL)**
Tahini sauce (*tarator*, p. 68) or
   tomato sauce (p. 139)
Fried pine nuts or almonds
Lemon wedges
Fresh herbs, to garnish

Rinse the fish with cold water, pat dry, and rub inside and out with the salt.

In a food processor or a mortar and pestle, pound the pine nuts until coarsely ground, but not a paste. Transfer to a bowl. Place the garlic, coriander, and a pinch of salt in your food processor or mortar and mash to a paste, then add it to the nuts in the bowl, along with the cilantro, onion, pepper, tomato, olive oil, lemon juice, cumin, black pepper, and Aleppo pepper or cayenne. Mix thoroughly.

Preheat the oven to 400°F (200°C) and grease a large baking dish with olive oil. Place the fish in the dish and cut slashes into the sides of the fish to help it cook evenly. Fill the cavity with the stuffing, wrapping any leftover stuffing up in a parcel of foil. Stitch the cavity shut using butcher's twine, if possible. Place the parcel of foil next to the fish and bake for 20 to 25 minutes or until the flesh is firm and opaque and separates easily from the bone (check inside the cut, at the thickest part of the fish). Leave to rest for 5 minutes. Remove the skin, if you wish. Serve hot with your chosen accompaniments.

# Rice with Chicken

## *Roz a' Djej*

My mother-in-law has served this classic Lebanese dish for family gatherings over the years. My husband's family is made up of five children, all married, with 3 or 4 children each. When we get together, it's very noisy but filled with so much love. In *roz a' djej*, tender chicken is served with rice cooked with delicately spiced ground beef and topped with toasted nuts. On special occasions, the rice mixture is used to stuff a whole chicken before roasting. When you make this dish your whole house will smell so good and welcoming.

1 tablespoon clarified butter
  or butter

4 tablespoons extra-virgin olive oil

1 lb (450 g) ground beef

½ teaspoon ground allspice

Pinch freshly ground black pepper

½ teaspoon ground cinnamon

Pinch freshly ground nutmeg

½ teaspoon ground caraway

2 cups (400 g) long-grain white rice

½ cup (70 g) pine nuts

½ cup (60 g) slivered almonds

½ cup (60 g) shelled pistachios

Plain yogurt, to serve (optional)

**CHICKEN AND BROTH**

5 lb (2.25 kg) free-range whole
  chicken or chicken pieces

1 large onion, quartered

1 cinnamon stick

2–3 allspice berries

2–3 black peppercorns

1–2 bay leaves

1 tablespoon coarse sea salt

Prepare the chicken and broth: Place the chicken in a large pot and cover with 4 quarts (4 liters) of water. Bring to a boil, skimming any foam from the surface. Add the onion, cinnamon stick, allspice, peppercorns, bay leaves, and salt. Reduce the heat and simmer until the chicken is cooked, 45 minutes. Reserving the broth, transfer the chicken to a chopping board until cool enough to handle, then pick the meat off the bones, and cut it into bite-size pieces. Place the chicken in a small pot with 1 cup (240 ml) of the broth so it doesn't dry out. Strain the remaining broth through a fine sieve and set aside.

In a large pot, heat the clarified butter and 1 tablespoon of the oil over medium heat. Add the beef, breaking it up with a wooden spoon, and cook until well browned. Stir in the spices and rice until evenly mixed. Add 4 cups (950 ml) of the reserved chicken broth (keeping the rest for use in other dishes). Bring to a boil, then reduce the heat, cover the pot, and simmer for 25 to 30 minutes, until the rice is tender. Remove from the heat and let stand for 5 minutes before fluffing with a fork.

Meanwhile, in a small frying pan, fry the pine nuts with 1 tablespoon of oil until golden brown. Using a slotted spoon, transfer to a plate lined with paper towels. In the same pan, fry the almonds, then the pistachios, adding them to the pine nuts on the plate.

If needed, reheat the chicken. Spoon the rice onto a large serving plate and top with the chicken pieces. Garnish with the nuts and serve hot, with plain yogurt and salad on the side, if you like.

# Baked Kafta with Potatoes

## *Kafta bi Saniyeh*

This dish is a family favorite in Lebanon. My husband grew up eating this dish and craves it whenever he is in the mood for comfort food. What you eat as a child stays in your sensual memory and, as you grow, you seek to bring those flavors back (remember that famous scene with the food critic in the movie *Ratatouille*?). *Kafta bi saniyeh* is not complicated to make. Some spread the ground meat mixture (*kafta*) evenly on the base of the baking dish, while others will form round patties to line the dish. The *kafta* is then topped with baked or fried potatoes and tomatoes, and cooked in a warm tomato sauce.

4 medium potatoes, sliced
  ¼ in (6 mm) thick

3 medium tomatoes, sliced

1 tablespoon tomato paste diluted
  with 2 tablespoons of water

1 cup (240 ml) chicken or beef stock

¼ teaspoon freshly ground
  black pepper

Vegetable oil, for greasing

Salt

**KAFTA**

1 lb (450 g) ground beef with 20% fat

2 oz (50 g) lamb fat (optional)

1 medium onion, very finely
  chopped

½ teaspoon ground allspice

1 teaspoon salt

Pinch freshly ground black pepper

1 small bunch flat-leaf parsley,
  finely chopped by hand

Make the *kafta*: If you can, ask your butcher to coarsely grind the meat with the fat, or use a food processor to pulse them together. In a mixing bowl, combine the chopped onion, allspice, salt, and pepper. Place the meat on a clean work surface and mix in the chopped parsley and onion mixture. Knead until evenly mixed.

Preheat the oven to 400°F (200°C) and grease a 9 by 13 in (23 by 33 cm) baking dish with oil. With moistened hands, spread the meat mixture evenly in the base, or form the mixture into evenly sized patties about ¾ in (2 cm) thick and arrange them in the dish in one layer. Bake for 20 minutes, until the meat is cooked.

Remove from the oven and lower the temperature to 375°F (190°C). Sprinkle the potatoes with salt and brush them with vegetable oil. Line a baking pan with parchment paper and arrange the potatoes on the pan in one layer. Bake for 30 minutes, flipping the potatoes halfway through. (Alternatively, you can deep-fry them.)

Top the meat in the dish with the sliced potatoes, followed by a layer of tomatoes.

In a mixing bowl, combine the diluted tomato paste with the stock, ¼ teaspoon salt, and the pepper. Pour into the baking dish. Cover the dish with foil, and bake for about 40 minutes, until hot and cooked through. Remove the foil for the last 10 minutes to brown the top. Serve hot with rice, Vermicelli Rice (p. 177), or Arabic bread (p. 28).

# Wheat Porridge with Lamb

## *Hrisseh*

*Hrisseh* is a thick wheat stew made with lamb or chicken (see Variation). Hearty, nourishing, and delicious, it is often cooked to distribute to those in need during religious times of almsgiving. The Christian community make *hrisseh* on Assumption Day, which celebrates Virgin Mary's bodily ascent to heaven at the end of her earthly life; while the Muslim community make it for Ashoura—the tenth day of Muharram, the first month of the Islamic calendar. It is also considered to be one of Armenia's national dishes.

I had my first taste of *hrisseh* when I was a child. A friend of my father's sent him some from a celebration in the village of Daraya in the Kesserouan district northeast of Beirut. Ever since, I have been searching for that particular chewy, rich taste. Many years later, upon my return to Lebanon after living the United States, I was invited to a community Easter celebration in Anjar, a town located in the Bekaa Valley with a large Armenian population. Huge cauldrons full of *hrisseh* were slowly boiling over a wood fire, under the supervision of a few people who took turns stirring. I remembered the taste immediately and was so grateful to have found it again. And I was moved that the whole community came together to share this meal.

Some years ago, I hosted a picnic for a large group of friends in Arsoun, in the Metn area, east of Beirut, and enlisted the help of Hisham and Nawal Hariz. This hospitable couple are small-scale food producers at Souk el Tayeb, Lebanon's first farmers' market. I asked them to make *hrisseh* for us as we picnicked in a beautiful forest near an ancient bridge, and they kindly shared their recipe. Look for pearled wheat berries (which cook faster than whole wheat berries) at Middle Eastern grocery stores, or substitute pearl barley.

2¼ lb (1 kg) boneless lamb shank, cut into chunks

8 oz–1 lb (225–450 g) lamb bones (depending on how rich you like it)

2 bay leaves

1 cinnamon stick

1 tablespoon coarse sea salt

½ teaspoon black peppercorns

2 cups (400 g) pearled wheat berries (or use pearl barley), soaked in cold water overnight

In a large stockpot, combine the meat, bones, spices, salt, and pepper with enough water to generously cover them. Bring to a boil over medium-high heat, skimming the foam from the surface. Reduce the heat, partially cover, and simmer for 1½ to 2 hours, adding more water if it dries, until you have a rich broth. Strain through a sieve, reserving the broth, meat, and bones.

In a large heavy pot, combine the meat and pearled wheat berries, and add the bones for a richer flavor. Pour in the stock to cover the wheat berries by 2 in (5 cm), topping it up with water if necessary. Bring to a boil, then reduce the heat and simmer for 1½ to 2 hours, stirring continuously to break apart the wheat, adding additional stock or water if it dries. The meat will dissolve into the wheat. You should have a thick, porridge-like consistency that is chewy and robust. Serve warm in bowls.

**Variation** In place of lamb, you can use a 5 lb (2.25 kg) chicken to make your broth. Shred the meat before adding it to the wheat. For extra richness, you can add lamb bones or melted butter or clarified butter to the wheat as it cooks.

# Upside-Down Rice

## *Maqloubeh*

Throughout its history, Lebanon has inherited many cross-cultural food traditions. *Maqloubeh* is a Palestinian dish also cooked in other neighboring countries, like Syria, Jordan, and Iraq. If you want to show off your wit and skills in the kitchen, *maqloubeh* is the perfect dish.

Flavorful meat, rice, and vegetables are layered in a pot, cooked, then flipped over onto a serving plate, the act that gives the dish its name (*maqloubeh* means upside down). If all is done just right, the dish holds the shape of the pot, showcasing neat layers. Friends and family gather to watch the moment of suspense and give the cook an ovation when the pot is lifted. Lately, many have been showcasing their flipping skills on social media. The recipe is versatile and can be made with chicken, fish, or simply vegetables in place of the meat. The vegetables can be varied as well; use eggplants and tomatoes during summer and cauliflower during the winter. This is my version, but feel free to experiment to create your own.

3 tablespoons extra-virgin olive oil

1 lb (450 g) boneless lamb shank, cut into chunks

1 onion, quartered

1–2 bay leaves

1 cinnamon stick

2–3 allspice berries

1 tablespoon coarse sea salt

½ cup (70 g) pine nuts (optional)

½ cup (65 g) slivered almonds (optional)

1 lb (450 g) ground beef or lamb

1 teaspoon ground allspice

¼ teaspoon freshly ground black pepper

¼ teaspoon ground cinnamon

1 teaspoon fine salt

2¼ lb (1 kg) eggplants

Vegetable oil, for frying

2–3 tomatoes, sliced

1 cup (200 g) long-grain white rice, rinsed and drained

In a large pot, heat 1 tablespoon of the olive oil and sear the lamb until browned. Add enough water to cover and bring to a boil, skimming the foam from the surface. Add the onion, bay leaves, cinnamon stick, allspice, and salt. Reduce the heat, cover, and simmer for 1 ½ to 2 hours, until the meat is very tender (you can do this in a pressure cooker, if you have one, to save time). Strain the broth through a fine sieve and set the meat and broth aside.

In a nonstick frying pan, fry the pine nuts and almonds separately, each with 1 tablespoon of olive oil, until golden brown. Using a slotted spoon, transfer to a plate lined with paper towels and set aside. In the same pan, add the ground meat, ground spices, and fine salt and cook for 10 minutes over medium heat, breaking the meat up with a wooden spoon, until browned. Mix in half of the fried nuts, reserving the rest for a garnish.

Cut off and discard the eggplant stems. Peel off the skin in alternating strips so the eggplants have a striped appearance. Cut them into lengthwise slices. Sprinkle both sides with salt and set aside in a colander for 30 minutes to drain excess moisture. Rinse and pat dry with paper towels.

Pour vegetable oil into a large pot or deep-fryer to a depth of 2 in (5 cm). Heat until the oil reaches a temperature of 350°F (180°C), or until small bubbles gather around a small piece of bread dropped into the oil. Working in batches, deep-fry the eggplant slices for 3–4 minutes until golden brown. Using a slotted spoon, transfer to a colander to drain excess oil.

Arrange the tomato slices to cover the base of a large Dutch oven or heavy nonstick cooking pot. Top with half of the ground meat in an even layer. Top with half of the eggplant slices, arranged to evenly cover the meat. Top with half of the lamb pieces, followed by the drained rice. Add another layer of the remaining ground meat, then the remaining eggplant slices, then the remaining lamb. Add 2 cups (480 ml) of the reserved broth. Bring to a boil, then reduce the heat, cover, and simmer for 25 to 30 minutes, until the rice is cooked. Leave to cool in the pot for at least 10 minutes—this will help achieve a neat shape when you flip.

When ready to serve, place a large dish on top of the pot. Holding it firmly in place, flip the pot over, and carefully lift the pot. Garnish the top with the remaining fried nuts before serving.

# Green Beans in Oil

## *Loubiyeh bi Zeit*

Tender green beans and ripe tomatoes are cooked in extra-virgin olive oil to make this simple, wholesome dish. You can go wild with the garlic or be shy and use two or three cloves. Either way is good. In the summer, I make this at least once a week with the tastiest green beans harvested from my father-in-law's garden. A friend once told me it was the best *loubiyeh bi zeit* he had ever had. I knew the reason, but let's keep it between us. The secret to good food is always to start with the best ingredients. When trimming the green beans, sit down and enjoy the work. Your children can help too. It's an opportunity to relax together and chat about life. Serve *loubiyeh bi zeit* with Arabic bread (p. 28) as a vegetarian meal.

2¼ lb (1 kg) green beans

¼ cup (60 ml) extra-virgin olive oil, plus extra for drizzling

2 garlic cloves–1 garlic bulb, minced or left whole (to your taste)

1 onion, finely chopped

½ teaspoon ground allspice

1 lb (450 g) ripe tomatoes, peeled and finely chopped

1 tablespoon tomato paste, diluted in 1 cup (240 ml) water

Salt and freshly ground black pepper

Trim the ends of the green beans and remove the strings. You can cut the beans in half or leave them whole. Wash and dry in a colander.

Heat the oil in a large pot over medium heat. If you are keeping your garlic cloves whole, add them to the oil and fry just until golden brown, watching carefully so they don't burn. Remove the garlic cloves using a slotted spoon and set aside. Add the onions to the pot and sauté until translucent. If using minced garlic, add it now. Stir in the green beans, followed by the allspice. Mix well, cover the pot, turn the heat to low, and let the beans steam for 5 minutes. Add the chopped tomatoes, diluted tomato paste, and fried garlic cloves (if using) and season with salt and pepper to taste. Cook for about 25 minutes, until tender but not overcooked. Remove from the heat and let cool. Drizzle with plenty of olive oil before serving at room temperature.

# Okra in Oil

## *Bamiyeh bi Zeit*

You either love okra or you don't! I shout my love of okra from the rooftops, especially prepared this way—hearty and full of flavor. Use only the freshest okra, in season, of course. The okra can be deep-fried before using to reduce the slimy texture that sometimes deters people. Some cooks add a dash of lemon juice or pomegranate molasses to the simmering pot for the same purpose. I usually don't do either—I never found that it made much of a difference. I like to sprinkle the dish with fresh cilantro at the end, but you can also add it halfway through the simmering time. Serve this dish with Arabic bread (p. 28) as a vegetarian meal.

1 tablespoon vegetable oil

1 tablespoon extra-virgin olive oil, plus extra for drizzling

1 onion, finely chopped

2 garlic cloves–1 garlic bulb, minced (to your taste)

2¼ lb (1 kg) small whole okra, stems trimmed if long

½ teaspoon ground allspice

1 teaspoon salt

4–5 firm red tomatoes, finely chopped

1 tablespoon tomato paste diluted in 1 cup (240 ml) water

1 small cinnamon stick

1 bunch cilantro, leaves finely chopped, to serve

Heat the oils in a large pot over medium heat. Sauté the onion until translucent, then add the garlic and cook until fragrant. Add the okra and sprinkle in the allspice and salt. Cover and simmer over low heat for about 3 minutes, until they begin to soften. Add the tomatoes, diluted tomato paste, and cinnamon stick and bring to a boil. Reduce the heat, partially cover, and simmer for about 25 minutes, until the okra is cooked but not too soft, and the sauce has thickened. Serve warm or at room temperature, garnished with chopped cilantro and a drizzle of olive oil.

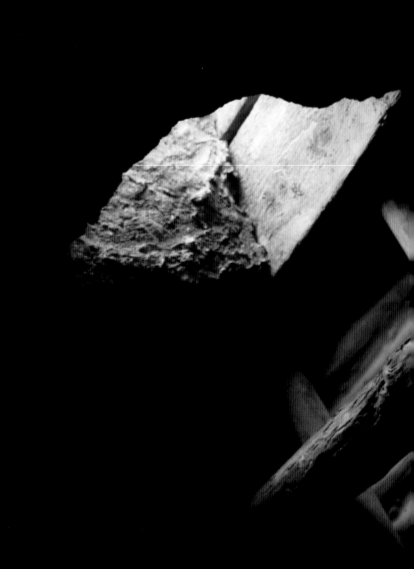

# PRESERVES & PANTRY STAPLES

# PRESERVES & PANTRY STAPLES
## *Mouneh*

A country's identity is based on many things, not the least of which is how its people feed themselves. Home-preserving seasonal foods for later use—preparing the *mouneh*—is an indelible part of our shared history as Lebanese. The typical Lebanese home was built in a way that included the storing of the *mouneh*. Large silos with big openings were built, each compartment designated for a type of food. In the wall cavities, jars were stored for safekeeping. The subject of *mouneh* has always fascinated me. I spent five years traveling throughout the country researching Lebanese preserves to write my book, *Mouneh: Preserving Foods for the Lebanese Pantry*, with recipes, stories, and photographs of the people and preserves I encountered.

The word *mouneh* comes from the Arabic word *mana*, meaning "storing." The idea evokes a feeling of home, security, nourishment, tradition, maternal instinct, and so much more. Recipes are passed down from one generation to another. In the past, especially in remote villages in Lebanon, the *mouneh* was prepared during summer's bountiful harvest for consumption during winter's harsh days. It was called *maswam el mouneh*. Those who did not own land, usually city dwellers, would wait for the best prices to buy all their goods to make their yearly *mouneh*.

*Mouneh* products provided fundamental nourishment of the daily meal, having transformed perishable produce into food with a long shelf life. Today, without the urgent necessity of preserving food for the winter, the *mouneh* has become more of a social tradition. For some, it is a way to keep our basic culinary heritage alive. For others, it is a conscious effort to avoid waste. Still, others continue to prepare *mouneh* for security purposes, as a safeguard against hunger in times of political instability, which unfortunately never seems to end. Though the intent may vary, the basic idea remains—food preservation.

Preparing one's *mouneh* is an elaborate task and in yesteryears sometimes involved a whole community. The main processes of production are done by concentration through evaporation, drying, and fermentation.

**Left:** A cat in Beirut watching street life unravel.

# Yogurt

## *Laban*

In the Lebanese tradition, yogurt is eaten at nearly every meal. It is served as an accompaniment to hearty main dishes such as stuffed vegetables, kibbeh, and rice-based dishes, and it is a central ingredient in many sauces and mezze dishes. It is also strained to make the Lebanese staple, labneh (p. 94). Traditionally, yogurt is made at home using farm-fresh goat milk, though cow milk works just as well if you prefer. If you source your milk from a farm, you can pasteurize it yourself using the instructions below. You will need a thermometer for best results, and can half this recipe for a smaller batch.

1 gallon (4 liters) milk
1 cup (250 g) plain yogurt with
    active cultures (starter)

Place the milk in a large heavy-based pot and heat to a temperature of 112°F (45°C). Turn off the heat and gently stir in the yogurt starter until it is thoroughly mixed. Cover the pot with a lid and wrap it with a woolen blanket to keep warm. Set the pot somewhere warm and free of drafts (the internal temperature should stay above 122°F/50°C) without disturbing it for 6 to 12 hours, until the yogurt sets. When the yogurt sets, uncover and pour the yogurt into an earthenware jar with a tight-fitting lid (or another airtight container). Chill for at least 6 hours in the refrigerator before eating it or using it to make labneh. After this point, you can transfer 1 cup (250 g) of yogurt to an airtight glass jar and refrigerate it to use as the starter for your next yogurt preparation. Store your yogurt in the refrigerator and use within 4 to 5 days.

**Note** If you are using unpasteurized milk, first strain the milk through cheesecloth to remove any impurities. To pasteurize, pour the liquid into a heavy pot and heat until it reaches a temperature of 200°F (95°C). Maintain this temperature for 30 minutes, until it begins to rise and froth forms around the edges. Stir frequently to prevent a skin from forming. To cool it down, cover the pot and place it in a larger receptacle of clean cold water until the milk reaches a temperature of 112°F (45°C). Proceed as above.

# Lebanese Lamb Confit

## *Awarma*

Up until about the 1960s, in villages all around Lebanon, a fat-tail sheep would be force-fed for months before the cold winter, following an ancient tradition shared by the entire population irrespective of ethnicity or religion. The sheep's main food source was vines and mulberry leaves. The sheep would be fed enough to grow to three times his original size, with a huge tail full of fat called *leeyeh*. In mid-September, the sheep would be slaughtered. The day of the slaughter was a big event in the village. Tables were set for a feast with an assortment of local dishes, including dishes requiring raw meat (see pp. 78, 111, and 112). Every part of the sheep was used, and meat was ground and preserved in fat to make *awarma* for consumption throughout the year. Today, *awarma* is still prepared, not so much for meat preservation, but for the exquisite flavor that the recipe provides. It is a prized ingredient, often used as a substitute for fresh meat in soups, stuffed vegetables, and kibbeh, and as a topping for baked flatbread (see p. 28). It is also typically fried with eggs in a traditional *fekhar*—a circular pottery cooking vessel (see p. 86). *Awarma* is robust mountain food—a small mouthful brings back childhood memories of endless summers in the family house high in the mountains—days of pure *dolce farniente* (sweet idleness). A little bit goes a long way.

8 oz (250 g) lamb fat, coarsely chopped
4 oz (115 g) lamb, finely ground or chopped into bite-size pieces
½ teaspoon coarse sea salt
1 small onion, unpeeled (optional)
1 allspice berry (optional)
1 small cinnamon stick (optional)
1 bay leaf

Heat 1 or 2 tablespoons of water in a heavy bottomed sauté pan (this will prevent the fat from sticking to the surface). Once the liquid has almost evaporated, add the lamb fat and cook over medium heat for a few minutes until it melts and the fat has rendered.

Add the meat and salt to the liquid fat in the pan, breaking up the pieces with a wooden spoon. If desired, add the onion (which reduces scum and adds flavor), allspice berry, cinnamon stick, and bay leaf. Cook, stirring constantly, for 10 to 15 minutes, until the meat is thoroughly and evenly cooked. Remove the onion pieces, allspice berry, bay leaf, and cinnamon stick, if used, and transfer the meat and fat to a clean jar or container. Allow to cool fully before covering. Store in the refrigerator.

# Labneh Balls in Oil

## *Labneh Mouka'zaleh bi Zeit*

Small balls of strained thickened yogurt (*labneh*) preserved in olive oil, green tangy olives, and a small bowl of *za'atar* mixed with olive oil is fundamental fare on the traditional Lebanese table. Goat milk labneh is traditional for this recipe, but cow milk labneh also works great. You can roll the balls in spices or herbs to enhance the flavor. Before you start, make sure your labneh is very thick, about the texture of cream cheese.

2 cups (450 g) Labneh (Thick
   Strained Yogurt, p. 94)
Extra-virgin olive oil, to cover
   (about 2 cups/480 ml)

**OPTIONAL FLAVORINGS
   (CHOOSE ONE OR A FEW)**
Crumbled dried mint
Dried cayenne or Aleppo pepper
*Za'atar* (see p. 31)
Nigella seeds
Cumin seeds
Dried edible rose petals
Toasted ground nuts

Line a tray with a clean piece of cheesecloth. Moisten your hands with a few drops of olive oil and place 1 heaped tablespoon of labneh into the palm of your hand. Roll into a ball about 1½ in (4 cm) in diameter and place on the lined tray. Repeat until you have used all of the labneh. Once all the balls have been formed, cover them with another sterilized cloth; this will ensure that the cheese balls dry sufficiently. Set aside in the refrigerator overnight, or until firm.

The next morning, place your chosen flavorings on separate plates and roll each labneh ball in one of the flavorings of your choice until lightly coated. Or you can leave them plain. You can serve them now, drizzled in olive oil, or transfer them to a clean wide-mouth jar or container, leaving enough space at the top to make sure they can be fully submerged.

Pour in enough olive oil to cover the balls completely and cover with a lid. Traditional practice is to store these in a cool, dark place, but refrigerate them to alleviate safety concerns (bring back to room temperature before serving). As you eat them, replenish the jars with olive oil.

# Red Pepper Paste

## *Ribb el Harr*

Once you start using red pepper paste in your cooking, it becomes addictive. I use it often. My youngest daughter, Sarah, once complained that our food was always too spicy, but when I omitted the paste in our next meal, she quickly changed her mind and asked me to add it back. Sarah had another opportunity to develop her taste for red pepper paste growing up: She and her cousin Alexia once kept us awake all night with their chatter and laughter. In my tired state the next day, I served them lentil soup with an almost punitive amount of red pepper paste. To this day, we still laugh about it.

To make the perfect red pepper paste for you and your family to enjoy, you must determine the ratio you like of hot peppers to sweet peppers. Some may prefer to use only hot peppers, though it's a bit daring. Others prefer to use only sweet peppers to make the paste. Sweet pepper paste is a great substitute for tomato paste and can be used for coating chicken, as a topping for *man'oushé* (see p. 35), or to flavor stews. I usually make red pepper paste with an even ratio of hot peppers to sweet. It is hot enough to be spicy, but sweet enough to eat without burning. You can double or triple this recipe if, like me, you can't get enough of it (my yearly batch requires 20 kg of peppers!).

Traditionally, the pepper purée would be cooked in large cauldrons, then laid out in the hot sun for a few days to dry. If you live in a dry sunny climate and would like to try your hand at this method, use an offset spatula to spread the puréed peppers onto a clean baking sheet in a thin, even layer. Cover with fine cheesecloth to protect them from insects or falling debris, and set the tray in full sun for 3 to 4 days, until dried to a thick paste, bringing it inside at the night to avoid exposing it to humidity.

4 lb 6 oz (2 kg) sweet red peppers
4 lb 6 oz (2 kg) hot red peppers
1 tablespoon salt

Rinse and drain the peppers. Using latex gloves to protect your hands, slit the peppers in half, removing the stems and seeds.

Bring a large pot of salted water to a boil and add the peppers. Return to a boil and cook for 10 to 15 minutes until tender. They are done when the skin falls off easily. Drain the peppers, squeezing out excess moisture, and set aside to dry.

Using a food processor or food mill, grind the peppers to a purée. Add the salt. Return to the pot and bring the mixture to a gentle boil. Cook, stirring constantly, until you have a thick paste, 10 to 15 minutes. Transfer to a clean jar or jars, waiting to cover until it has cooled fully. This keeps in the fridge for a couple of months, depending on how carefully it is stored, or you can freeze it in portions.

# Red Pepper Marinade

To make a delicious marinade for meat, chicken, or fish, crush 2 garlic cloves and finely chop ½ bunch of cilantro. Fry the garlic in 1 to 2 tablespoons of extra-virgin olive oil, add the cilantro, and cook for 1 minute until fragrant. Mix this paste with 1 to 2 tablespoons of red pepper paste, the juice of 1 lemon, and ¼ cup (60 ml) of extra-virgin olive oil. Use to marinate about 2¼ lb (1 kg) meat, chicken, or fish.

# Pickled Turnips

## *Kabees Lefet*

Large jars of rose-colored pickled turnips (made pink from the addition of beets) decorate the front counters of restaurants and snack shops all around Lebanon and throughout the Levant. Pickled turnips are easy to make and very tasty. They are often present on the mezze table, and an essential side to falafel and shawarma. They can also be served alongside meat or vegetable stews, grills, or simply added to your favorite sandwich or topped flatbread (see p. 25). You can halve or double this recipe to your liking.

2¼ lb (1 kg) small white turnips

1 medium beet

1 chile pepper or a few thyme
  sprigs per jar

**PICKLING SOLUTION**

4 cups (1 liter) water

2 cups (480 ml) vinegar
  (with 5% acidity)

⅓ cup (75 g) coarse sea salt

Make the pickling solution: In a nonreactive pot, combine the salt and water and boil until the salt has completely dissolved. Turn off the heat and let cool until the liquid is room temperature. Strain the liquid through a fine sieve lined with a piece of sterilized cheesecloth, mix in the vinegar, and set aside. (Any unused solution can be stored in a sterilized jar in a cool dark place for up to two weeks.)

Wash the turnips very well and pat them dry. Trim the ends and peel the turnips. Pull out any thin roots on the skin. The pieces should be spotless. Without separating the pieces from the root, cut 4 deep slices into the turnip at even intervals (for whole pickled turnips). Alternatively, cut them into batons. Peel the beet and cut it into quarters or even pieces.

Pack the turnip into a clean jar or jars, interspersing them with beet slices (you may not fit them all at this stage). Place a chile pepper or a few thyme sprigs into each jar. Pour in enough pickling solution to completely cover the contents of the jar. Leave the pickles to settle for 10 minutes, then top up the jars with more turnips and pickling solution, leaving ½ inch (1 cm) of space at the top. This will prevent the turnips from floating in the liquid. Cover and screw on the lid tightly.

Store in the refrigerator for 2 to 3 weeks before consuming.

# Pickled Green Olives

## *Kabees Zeitoon 'Akhdar*

In Lebanon, olives are sometimes referred to as "the sheikh of the table," an expression that reveals their importance. It is also common to hear the expression "eating bread and olives" which means going back to the basics in life. A small plate of olives is almost always present on the table during meals, often alongside bread, local cheeses, or a plate of *labneh* (see p. 94) drizzled with olive oil. These are life's simple pleasures.

Green olives are picked young and have a dense, sharp flavor. When purchasing or collecting raw olives for this recipe, select small, firm fruits that have been harvested by hand for best results. Green olives can be cured using different methods, and pickled whole, crushed, or slit. Depending on the technique used, olives will have a different flavor, texture, and curing time. This is the traditional method in Lebanon.

2¼ lb (1 kg) fresh green-ripe olives

1–2 lemons, rinsed, unpeeled
   and sliced

1 red or green chile pepper
   (optional), rinsed and drained

Fresh thyme sprigs (optional),
   rinsed and drained

Bay leaves (optional)

Extra-virgin olive oil

1 twig from a bitter orange, lemon,
   or olive tree (optional)

**BRINE**

8 cups (2 liters) water

¾ cup (210 g) coarse sea salt

**MARINADE, TO SERVE**

2 parts extra-virgin olive oil

1 part freshly squeezed lemon juice

Pick through the olives, removing any twigs or debris, and wash them well under cold running water. Drain. You may keep the olives whole, crush each one with a clean stone or a heavy pestle to burst the flesh open, or alternatively, slit each olive lengthwise on both sides using a sharp knife or a razor blade (this will impact the brining time).

Put the prepared olives in a large bowl or basin, cover with water, and leave to soak for 5 to 7 days, depending on the bitterness of your variety, changing the water twice daily and ensuring they are covered in water at all times. Drain.

Once the olives have been soaked, clean your jar or jars. Make the brine: In a nonreactive pot, combine the salt and water and boil until the salt has completely dissolved. Turn off the heat and let cool until the liquid is room temperature. Strain the liquid through a fine sieve lined with a piece of sterilized cheesecloth and set aside. (Any unused solution can be stored in a sterilized jar in a cool dark place for up to two weeks.)

Pack the olives into your jar or jars, interspersing them with the lemon slices and the chile peppers, thyme sprigs, and bay leaves, if using. Add the brine to completely cover the contents of the jar. Pour in a thin layer of olive oil. Place twigs on top of the olives in the jar to keep them immersed in the brine; these will also give the olives a subtle flavor too. Screw on the lid, wipe the jars with a damp kitchen towel, and store, traditionally in a cool dark place but refrigerate to alleviate safety concerns. Whole olives should sit for best at least 6 months before consumption. Slit olives are best after at least 2 months. Crushed olives are best after at least 1 month.

To serve, drain the brine and mix the olives with the marinade.

# Apricot Jam

## *Mrabba el Meshmosh*

Apricot jam is often eaten with bread for breakfast, or after a large meal. If you live in an area where there is plenty of sun and low humidity, you can make this jam the traditional Lebanese way. Boil the ingredients together for 10 minutes then spread across a cheesecloth-lined tray. Leave the tray in the hot summer sun for 7 to 10 days, depending on weather conditions, bringing it inside overnight to avoid exposure to humidity.

2 lb (1 kg) apricots
2½ cups (500 g) sugar
Juice of 1 lemon

Rinse the apricots under cold running water and dry with a clean kitchen towel. Using a sharp knife, cut each fruit in half lengthwise following the natural line. Firmly grasp the two halves and twist them in opposite directions. Pull them apart and remove the pit.

In a large glass bowl, layer the sugar and apricots, starting and finishing with a layer of sugar. Cover with a clean cloth and leave to stand overnight.

The next day, clean your jars in hot water. In a large nonreactive pot, combine the apricots, sugar, and lemon juice. Slowly bring to a boil. Boil gently for 30 to 35 minutes, stirring frequently and skimming any foam that forms on the surface, until the temperature reaches 220°F (105°C) and the jam has reached setting point. (If you don't have a thermometer, you can test this by popping a plate in the freezer—spoon a drop onto the cold plate and tilt it. You are aiming for a slow descent, not a runny mess.)

Transfer to a jar or container and allow to cool fully before covering securely and storing in the refrigerator.

# Pumpkin in Syrup

*Lakteen bil ʿAtr*

This is a delicious sweet dessert that is always welcome after a lavish Lebanese meal. Most Lebanese restaurants will offer diners a variety of similar preserves at the end of their meal, alongside seasonal fresh fruits. Serve this delicious pumpkin preserve with fresh fruit, local fresh cheese, and Arabic bread.

It is traditionally made using pickling lime, a food-grade calcium hydroxide used in many traditional pickling and preserve recipes to yield a crunchy texture. Pickling lime can be very dangerous if handled improperly, so if you choose to use it, use gloves and be sure to follow all of the safety precautions on your package very closely. If you omit it, your preserve won't have the same texture, and you will need to reduce the cooking time so the pumpkin pieces hold their shape. You can easily halve or double this recipe.

5 lb (2.25 kg) pumpkin or butternut squash, peeled and cut into 2 in (5 cm) cubes (you need 2 lb/1 kg prepared)

1 cup (120 g) food-grade pickling lime (optional)

3 cups (600 g) sugar

Juice of 1 lemon

**OPTIONAL FLAVORINGS (PICK ONE)**

1 vanilla bean

1 cinnamon stick

1 tablespoon orange blossom water

Read all safety procedures on your pickling lime package. Wearing gloves and taking extreme care, dissolve the pickling lime in 1 gallon (4 liters) of water in a large basin. Leave to rest for at least 2 hours. Filter the water through a sieve lined with a fine cloth into a clean basin. Soak the pumpkin pieces in the pickling lime solution overnight. The next day, drain and rinse the pumpkin pieces very thoroughly to remove any trace of pickling lime solution. Soak in fresh water for an additional 3 hours, changing the water 3 times. Drain and leave to dry completely.

In a large nonreactive pot, combine the sugar and 5 cups (1.2 liters) of water. Slowly bring to a boil, stirring constantly, and continue to stir and skim any foam from the surface for 10 to 15 minutes, until the sugar has dissolved and you have a syrup. Add the pumpkin pieces and the lemon juice to the sugar syrup and cook on low heat until the pumpkin is fork-tender but not soft, about 1 hour if you used pickling lime, or less time if you omitted it. Add your choice of flavoring in the last 5 minutes of cooking.

Carefully spoon the pumpkin pieces into clean jars or a heat-safe container and pour the syrup over to cover them completely. Serve immediately, or store in the refrigerator.

# SWEETS

# SWEETS

## *Helwayat*

"*Helwe wa morra* (sweet or sour)?" your hostess or host will shout out after a lavish Lebanese meal to ask how you would like your Arabic coffee. Coincidentally, this is the name of a show that ran on the national TV station LBC a few years ago. I hosted a weekly food segment showcasing traditional foods of Lebanon made mostly by small-scale producers, local cooks, and chefs. I traveled around the country to discover and share endangered recipes of our Lebanese culinary heritage. This corresponded well with my work with the Slow Food movement and our local chapter Slow Food Beirut, of which I am a founding member.

The coffee is served and sipped slowly by guests. Once done, cups are turned upside down on the saucer, turned three times, and left to settle for a few minutes. Crowds gather to hear what the designated coffee cup reader has to say about hidden messages disguised in the coffee grounds of the empty cup. I've taken great joy in entertaining my children's friends by reading their coffee cups. My daughter Sarah is often very surprised how well I can target her friends' personalities or bring up subjects that are so relevant to their lives. I am not a professional coffee reader, but I use my intuition based on a person's vibe. It's great fun, a ritual like reading your daily horoscope.

Sweets (*helwayat*) in Lebanon are very rich, and therefore rarely served after a meal. We all have a sweet tooth but will indulge in sweets during special occasions, religious events, a rite of passage, or when visiting friends or relatives. A few bites in the morning with our coffee is a perfect way to start the day. Fresh fruit or local jams are usually served to finish a meal in Lebanon.

A wide variety of sweets made in Lebanon are associated with the celebration of a specific holiday or event in one's life. Some sweets are easy to make at home, while others are traditionally left to specialists. Arabic pastry shops are abundant, mostly in big cities like Beirut, Tripoli, and Saida. During my culinary travels around the country, I have had the privilege to enter their kitchens and learn secrets of the trade. All are generous, both with their hospitality (mostly by stuffing me with so many delicious bites) and with their stories. These shops all carry experience and knowledge handed down from one generation to another.

An assortment of Lebanese sweets bought at a specialized pastry shop is often the first and best choice. The repertoire of sweets is vast. It includes puddings, pastries, cookies, ice cream, candied fruit, nuts, and jams. Some of the primary ingredients in Lebanese sweets are nuts—mainly pistachios, walnuts, almonds, and pine nuts. Spices include cinnamon, nutmeg, and cloves. The most distinct flavorings are orange blossom water and rose water, added to infuse sugar syrup, which is drizzled abundantly on top.

Friends or family never come empty-handed to someone's house when invited. Tradition in Lebanon says that one should come bearing gifts. Could there be a better time for this tradition than now?

**Left:** Rose water and orange blossom water are essential ingredients in most Lebanese sweets.

# Baklava

Baklava is one of the most popular sweets made in Lebanon and in neighboring countries, often associated with joyful occasions. There are many variations of baklava with different shapes, flavors, colors, and peculiarities. These are sold in specialty shops produced by artisans with generations of history, knowledge, and expertise, presented on an assortment of iron trays.

When working in my father's restaurant in Florida in the 1980s, this baklava was our best-selling dessert. We would receive trays every day from our head chef, Haygas, an Armenian immigrant. He and his wife skillfully prepared it in their Middle Eastern shop. The scent of warm baklava always brings me back to that special time in my life, in Florida at our family restaurant. You can find rose water and orange blossom water (not to be confused with extracts) in Middle Eastern stores and well-stocked supermarkets. I use Cortas brand.

3½ cups (400 g) chopped walnuts, pistachios, or a mixture

1 cup (200 g) sugar

1 tablespoon good-quality orange blossom water

1 tablespoon good quality rose water

16 oz (450 g) package phyllo pastry sheets, thawed

1 cup (225 g) unsalted butter, melted

½ teaspoon cinnamon (optional)

¼ cup (25 g) finely ground pistachios, to garnish

**SUGAR SYRUP**

*(makes about 2¾ cups/650 ml)*

3 cups (600 g) sugar

1½ cups (350 ml) water

2 tablespoons freshly squeezed lemon juice

1 teaspoon rose water

1 teaspoon orange blossom water

Place the nuts in a food processor with a little of the sugar and pulse until ground, but not a paste. Transfer to a mixing bowl and mix in the remaining sugar and the orange blossom and rose waters. Set aside.

Unwrap the phyllo pastry and cover it with a clean towel, keeping it covered as you work so it doesn't dry out. Ready a rectangular baking dish that is the same size of your pastry sheets and brush the bottom and sides with butter. Place one sheet of pastry in the base and brush the top with butter. Place another sheet on top, brushing again with butter. Repeat until you have used up half of the phyllo sheets.

Preheat the oven to 350°F (180°C). Spread the nut mixture evenly on top of the sheets in the dish. Sprinkle the top with cinnamon, if using. Continue stacking the remaining sheets on top, brushing each with butter. Brush the final sheet thinly with water before brushing with butter. Moisten a sharp knife with water and cut the pastry into even squares, diamond shapes, or bite-size pieces, keeping the knife moistened as you work.

Make the sugar syrup: In a saucepan, combine the sugar and water and place over medium heat. Stir until the sugar dissolves, then add the lemon juice and bring to a boil, stirring constantly. Lower the heat and simmer for an additional 10 minutes, until the it thickens to a syrup. Remove from the heat, let it cool, then stir in the rose water and orange blossom water. You should have about 2¾ cups (650 ml). You can store unused sugar syrup in a bottle for up to a week in the refrigerator to use in other recipes.

Bake the baklava for 20 minutes, or until the pastry is crisp and golden. Remove from the oven and, while still hot, pour cool sugar syrup all over. Garnish the top with ground pistachios and set aside for at least 1 hour to allow the syrup to soak in. Serve at room temperature.

# Stuffed Semolina Shortbread
## *Ma'amoul*

*Ma'amoul* are dense shortbread cookies filled with a sweetened filling—typically made with pistachios, walnuts, almonds, or dates. They are shaped in a traditional wooden mold called a *tabbeh* (pictured on facing page) and are most often associated with religious holidays, especially Easter, Eid al-Fitr, Eid al-Adha, and Ramadan. Easter *ma'amoul* are made in two shapes: the date ones are typically round to symbolize the crown of thorns, and the nut ones are oval shaped, symbolizing the sponge Christ was given to quench his thirst. Just before these holidays, mothers and daughters, neighbors, sisters, and cousins meet to engage in the very serious undertaking of making large quantities of *ma'amoul*, taking great pride in their own recipe and reputation. Once baked on trays, they are stored and distributed to family and friends, or served to guests with coffee or tea.

Mastic (Arabic gum) is a pale-yellow tree resin that has been harvested since ancient times to yield a chewy texture in foods. *Mahlab* is a spice with a delicate sweetness, made from the seeds of a species of cherry. You can find both in health food stores, well-stocked Middle Eastern grocery stores, or online.

### DOUGH

Generous ¾ cups (100 g) all-
   purpose flour

3 cups (500 g) coarse semolina

3 cups (500 g) fine semolina

¼ teaspoon-size piece of mastic
   (Arabic gum), optional, but find
   it if you can

¾ cup (150 g) sugar

1 teaspoon ground *mahlab*
   (optional)

½ teaspoon instant yeast

1¾ cups (400 g) unsalted butter
   or ghee, cubed

1 tablespoon orange blossom water

1 tablespoon rose water

Confectioners' sugar, for dusting

*Continued on next page*

Make the dough: In a large mixing bowl, combine the flour and coarse and fine semolina. In a mortar and pestle, crush the mastic with 1 tablespoon of the sugar until fine and incorporated. Tip it into the bowl of flours, along with the remaining sugar, *mahlab*, and yeast and mix well. Add the butter and use your fingers to mix it in until it resembles fine breadcrumbs. Add the orange blossom and rose waters and knead until you have a firm dough, about 10 minutes. Mix in a tablespoon of water, only if needed. Place the dough into a bowl, cover with a kitchen towel, and set aside at room temperature for 3 hours, or in the refrigerator overnight.

Next, make your fillings: In a mixing bowl, combine all of the nut filling ingredients, mix well, and set aside. In another mixing bowl, combine the dates and butter, then mix in the cinnamon, if using. Knead the date mixture until it comes together into a ball. Divide into about 35 teaspoon-size balls. Set aside.

Preheat the oven to 350°F (180°C), and line two large baking sheets with parchment paper.

Divide the dough in half—one half for the nut filling, and one for the date filling. Measure about 1 tablespoon of the dough and roll it into a ball. Flatten it in the palm of your hand. Place 1 heaped teaspoon of nut filling or 1 ball of date filling in the center, then fold the dough over the filling and roll it between your palms until it is evenly encased in dough. If you have a *ma'amoul* mold, use one shape for nut filling and another for date filling.

## NUT FILLING

1¾ cups (200 g) chopped walnuts,
  pistachios, or a mixture,
  pulsed in a food processor
  until finely chopped
¼ cup (50 g) sugar
½ teaspoon ground cinnamon
  (optional)
1½ teaspoon orange blossom water
1½ teaspoon rose water

## DATE FILLING

2 cups (250 g) pitted unsweetened
  dried dates, mashed (or use
  date paste)
1 tablespoon butter, at room
  temperature
Pinch ground cinnamon (optional)

Gently press the filled dough into the mold with your fingers until it is even with the surface of the mold (you can add a bit more dough, if needed). Slam the edge of the wooden mold face down on a hard surface until the shaped *ma'amoul* drops out. If you are shaping by hand, place the filled dough on the lined baking sheet and press indents into the top with a fork or pastry tongs. Repeat until you have used all of the dough and fillings, leaving 1 in (2.5 cm) of space between the *ma'amoul* on the baking sheets.

Bake for 20 minutes until very lightly golden on the bottom, but watch carefully so they don't over-bake. Cool on wire racks—they will firm up as they cool. Once cooled, dust the nut *ma'amoul* with confectioners' sugar (the date-filled ones don't require additional sweetening). Store in a cookie tin.

# Milk Pudding

## *Mhalabiyeh*

Milk pudding—a classic in our sweet repertoire—is a light, cool, comforting dessert that brings us back to childhood family gatherings. My grown children and I both have childhood memories of sneaking into the fridge to have a bowl. *Mhalabiyeh* can take on an array of flavors, depending on the topping you choose. The delicate flavors of orange blossom and rose water are undeniably important to make it a true Lebanese dessert, but you can top the pudding with an array of homemade jams or compotes, chopped nuts, shredded coconut, dried fruits, or a combination of these. It is also delicious simply sprinkled with cinnamon.

½ teaspoon-size piece of mastic
   (Arabic gum, see p. 216), optional
1 cup (200 g) sugar
½ cup (60 g) cornstarch
4 cups (1 liter) whole milk
1 tablespoon orange blossom
   water, or more to taste
1 tablespoon rose water, or more
   to taste

**TOPPINGS (OPTIONAL)**
Pinch ground cinnamon
1 cup (320 g) fruit jam or compote
Scant ½ cup (50 g) ground
   pistachios
Dried fruits or dried, shredded
   coconut

In a mortar and pestle, crush the mastic with 1 tablespoon of sugar until fine and combined.

Dissolve the cornstarch in ½ cup (120 ml) water and pour through a strainer into a heavy pot. Add the milk and bring to a boil, stirring constantly. Reduce the heat and simmer, still stirring, for 5 minutes. Add the remaining sugar and stir until completely dissolved. Stir in the ground mastic and simmer gently for 20 minutes until it thickens. Remove from heat and mix in the orange blossom water and rose water.

Divide the pudding equally among serving bowls and leave them to cool. Cover with plastic wrap and refrigerate for at least 4 hours until chilled and set.

Serve chilled, topped with your choice of toppings.

# Rice Pudding

*Roz bi Haleeb*

Rice pudding is a quick, easy, and fragrant recipe to make for family and friends. Keep some in the fridge for a quick snack to satisfy your sweet cravings, or serve it at the end of a light meal. It won't last long though—it can be addictive. I remember making rice pudding in Portugal as a food consultant for Ezzat, a restaurateur who was in the process of opening a charming Lebanese restaurant in Lisbon. As we made the pudding, Ezzat invited a friend or two. We couldn't stop tasting as the recipe developed. We were left with a negligible amount to refrigerate. Needless to say, we were satisfied with the results.

½ cup (100 g) short-grain white rice

1 teaspoon-size piece of mastic
   (Arabic gum, see p. 216), optional

1 cup (200 g) sugar

4 cups (1 liter) whole milk

1 tablespoon orange
   blossom water

1 tablespoon rose water

Scant ½ cup (50 g) ground
   pistachios, to garnish (optional)

Rinse the rice well, then soak in cold water for 1 hour.

In a mortar and pestle, crush the mastic with 1 tablespoon of the sugar until fine and combined. Drain the rice and place it in a heavy pot with 1 cup (240 ml) water. Bring to a boil, then reduce the heat, cover, and simmer for 10 minutes. Stirring constantly, slowly pour in the milk, followed by the remaining sugar. Add the ground mastic mixture to the pot and simmer for 45 minutes to 1 hour, until the rice is cooked and the mixture has thickened. Remove from the heat and mix in the orange blossom water and rose water. Divide the pudding equally among serving bowls and leave them to cool. Cover with plastic wrap and refrigerate for at least 4 hours until chilled and set.

Serve cold, garnished with ground pistachios.

# Stuffed Pancakes

## *Atayef*

For *atayef*, bite-size pancakes are stuffed with a cream filling, folded into a cone shape, decorated with chopped nuts or crystallized orange blossom petals, and served with a drizzle of sugar syrup. In another variation, the pancakes are stuffed with nuts, tightly sealed into a half-moon, deep-fried, and soaked in sugar syrup. *Atayef* is popularly eaten at sunset to break the fast during Ramadan, the Islamic month of fasting, or to celebrate the Christian St. Barbara's Day (*Eid il-Burbara*), which is our version of Halloween (though not related to the dead). Children wear disguises (as the patron saint did to flee the Romans who were persecuting her) and go around the neighborhood, dancing and singing the story of the revered saint and martyr. Each house will offer food and sometimes small gifts or money. Because my name is Barbara, children in school in the mid-'70s would tease me by circling around me and chanting "*Eid il-Burbara*," which made me cry.

2½ cups (300 g) all-purpose flour

½ teaspoon instant yeast

1 tablespoon sugar

¼ teaspoon salt

1 teaspoon baking powder

3 cups (700 ml) lukewarm water, plus extra, if needed

2 tablespoons vegetable oil or melted butter, plus extra for cooking the pancakes

2 cups (500 g) clotted cream or full-fat ricotta

Crystallized orange blossom petals, or ½ cup (50 g) very finely chopped pistachios, to garnish (optional)

Sugar syrup (p. 214), to serve

In a mixing bowl, combine the flour, yeast, sugar, salt, and baking powder. Gradually mix in the lukewarm water and oil or butter, whisking vigorously until you have a batter the consistency of thick cream. If it is too thick, whisk in water, one tablespoon at a time. Cover and let rest for at least 1 hour.

Spread a clean kitchen towel on a tray. You will place the cooked pancakes here to cool. Heat a tablespoon of oil or butter in a heavy, nonstick frying pan over medium-low heat. Whisk the batter again and, working in batches, pour in batter to make pancakes 4 inches (10 cm) in diameter. Cook without moving them until bubbles form on the surface, indicating that your batter is just right (if they don't, your batter is too thick—mix in a tablespoon of water and try again). Cook the pancakes without flipping for 2 to 3 minutes until the surface is dry, without any shine. Do not cook the other side; use a spatula to transfer them to the tray, brown side down, to cool. Cover the cooked pancakes with a clean kitchen towel while you make the rest, adding more oil or butter between batches if needed.

Place 1 tablespoon of clotted cream or ricotta in the center of the light side of a pancake. Gently fold into a semicircle and pinch the edges together halfway, forming a cone-like shape that is open at one end. Garnish the exposed filling with 2 or 3 crystallized orange blossom flowers, or dip it into ground pistachios. Repeat until all of the pancakes are filled. Serve immediately, drizzled with sugar syrup.

# Turmeric Cake

## *Sfouf*

Not quite a dessert, this colorful semolina cake is the perfect sweet bite for breakfast or an afternoon snack. In Lebanon, mothers who aren't at work might meet before their daily chores for a *sobhieh*—morning gathering. Cookies and *sfouf* will be presented to guests with a steaming pot of Arabic coffee or tea. *Sfouf* in Arabic translates to "a line," referring to the nuts lined up in neat rows across the cake. It is not too sweet and very easy to make at the last minute.

3 cups (500 g) fine semolina

1 cup (120 g) all-purpose flour

1 tablespoon baking powder

4 tablespoons ground turmeric

2 cups (400 g) sugar

1 cup (240 ml) vegetable oil or
   other neutral oil

2 cups (480 ml) whole milk

4 tablespoons tahini (or use butter)

2 tablespoons pine nuts or
   slivered almonds

In a mixing bowl, combine the semolina, flour, baking powder, and turmeric.

In another bowl, combine the sugar and oil and whisk until the sugar is dissolved. Add this to the dry ingredients and mix well. Gradually whisk in the milk to form a batter.

Preheat the oven to 350°F (180°C). Grease the bottom and sides of a 11 by 7 in (28 by 18 in) brownie pan with the tahini. Carefully pour the batter into the pan. Decorate the top of the batter with pine nuts or almonds, arranged in diagonal rows about 2 in (5 cm) apart.

Bake for 20 to 25 minutes or until a tester inserted in the center comes out clean. Remove and leave to cool in the pan. Using a sharp knife, cut into squares or diamonds, with the nuts in a line across the middle.

Store in a sealed container for up to 3 days.

# Spiced Rice Flour Pudding

## *Meghli*

One of the most special occasions in one's life is the birth of a child. Throughout Lebanon, *meghli* is made to celebrate the birth of a new baby. Rich in spices, made with rice flour, and topped with nuts, the pudding is said to bring the newborn good luck, nourish a breastfeeding mother, and help her with milk production. For at least a month, friends and relatives visit to meet the new baby and *meghli* will be made almost daily to serve guests and the new parents. It is typically the role of the grandmothers to make this dessert, but in my case, my husband took on this task when our first child was born. I can still remember him smiling over a huge pot as he patiently stirred the pudding. He felt very proud. I would eat a bowl every day. It is gluten-free and dairy-free. Be generous with the toppings or you might be judged accordingly by all of your guests!

1 cup (160 g) white rice flour

1½ cups (250 g) sugar

1 tablespoon ground caraway
  seeds

1 tablespoon ground cinnamon

1 tablespoon ground anise seeds

**TOPPINGS**

1¾ cups (200 g) halved or
  slivered almonds

1¾ cups (200 g) chopped walnuts

1 cup (100 g) chopped pistachios

1½ cups (210 g) pine nuts

⅔ cup (50) ground pistachios

⅔ cup (35 g) unsweetened
  shredded coconut

Soak the almonds, walnuts, pistachios, and pine nuts separately in cold water overnight. Drain and set aside.

In a large, heavy pot, mix the rice flour, sugar, caraway, cinnamon, and anise. Carefully pour in 8 cups (2 liters) of water and bring to a boil, stirring constantly. Reduce the heat to medium and simmer, stirring constantly, for 45 to 50 minutes, until thickened and cooked.

Divide the pudding equally among serving bowls and leave them to cool. Cover with plastic wrap and refrigerate for at least 4 hours until chilled and set.

Serve cold, topped with a generous sprinkling of nuts and shredded coconut.

# Wheat Porridge

## *Snayniyeh*

Wheat porridge is a nutritious dessert served to celebrate the first tooth of a child. The word "*snayniyeh*" is derived from the Arabic word "*snan*," which means teeth. Local superstition dictates that making this dessert will improve the appearance and health of your child's teeth. Notice that the grains of wheat resemble little teeth too. Traditionally, mothers would send a bowl of *snayniyeh* to friends, neighbors, and relatives at first sight of the tooth. The empty bowl would be returned with a small gift: a baby garment, a toy, a gold coin, fruit, or another type of sweet. *Snayniyeh* is often festively adorned with nuts, dried fruit, and crunchy, colorful sugar-coated chickpeas—a Turkish confection cherished by people of all ages in Lebanon. Look for sugared chickpeas and pearled wheat berries in Middle Eastern grocery stores or online.

1 cup (200 g) pearl wheat berries
   (or use pearl barley)
1 cup (200 g) sugar
2 tablespoons orange blossom
   water, or more to taste
2 tablespoons rose water,
   or more to taste

**TOPPINGS (CHOOSE
   YOUR FAVORITE)**
½ cup (50 g) chopped walnuts
½ cup (60 g) slivered or
   halved almonds
1½ cups (210 g) pine nuts
½ cup (50 g) pistachios,
   coarsely chopped
½ cup (80 g) raisins
8 oz (225 g) sugar-coated chickpeas
1 cup (180 g) pomegranate seeds

Soak the wheat berries in cold water overnight, or for at least 12 hours. Drain. Soak the nuts and raisins separately in water overnight (if using), drain, and set aside.

In a large pot, cover the wheat berries with about 8 cups (2 liters) of fresh water, bring to a boil, then reduce the heat and simmer for about 90 minutes, until cooked and tender, topping up the water as necessary. Alternatively, you can do this in a pressure cooker; it will take about 30 minutes.

Add the sugar and stir over low heat until it dissolves. Remove from the heat and mix in the orange blossom and rose waters.

Serve warm in bowls, sprinkled with your chosen toppings.

SERVES 12

# Turmeric Rice Pudding

## *Moufattaka*

**Moufattaka** is one of the oldest traditional desserts made in west Beirut—a specialty cherished by the Sunni community. It is very rich in flavor and can be quite labor intensive to make, since it requires hours of stirring the ingredients over the heat. I suggest you enlist a friend to help with the stirring. The name *moufattaka* translates to "unsewn," as the ingredients are elasticized during the process, resulting in a fragrant sticky pudding with a yellow tint. It is eggless, dairy-free, and gluten-free. The recipe makes a large quantity to reward you for the work, but you can halve it if you prefer.

The Makari family has been producing *moufattaka* for generations. I had the opportunity to learn how to make this rich dessert at their shop in Basta while filming a cooking segment for a local TV station in the '90s. They shared their secrets with generosity and transparency. The story began when the grandfather Hajj Abdallah, also known as the "King of Moufattaka," opened a sweet shop serving this yellow pudding in Basta around 1880. According to Hajj Makari (the current owner), before the civil war, families would bring *moufattaka* to the public beach in Ramlet al Bayda to celebrate the commemoration of the prophet Ya'oob (Job) on the last Wednesday of April. Children would fly kites and families would picnic. Unfortunately, this tradition has been lost and tall buildings have invaded the beautiful sandy beaches.

5 cups (1 kg) short-grain white rice

1 gallon (3.5 liters) water

5 tablespoons (50 g) ground turmeric

10 cups (2 kg) sugar

4 cups (1 kg) tahini

1 cup (140 g) pine nuts

Rinse the rice well and soak in cold water for 1 hour or overnight. Rinse, drain, and set aside.

Place the measured water in a large heavy pot, add the turmeric, and bring to a boil. Add the rice and boil, uncovered, until water evaporates to the level of the rice. Reduce the heat to very low, cover the pot, and simmer for 40 minutes until the rice has cooked down to a sticky mushy mixture. Set aside to cool.

In a large mixing bowl, combine the sugar, tahini, and pine nuts. Add the mixture to the rice and (now the work starts) cook over medium heat, stirring the mixture constantly with a wooden spoon to make sure the rice never sticks to the bottom of the pot. The more you stir the *moufattaka* the more elastic the texture will be. Cook for about 2 hours or until the oil from the tahini starts to separate from the mixture. This technique is called "*sarej*" in Arabic. It is an indication that the *moufattaka* is ready.

Remove from the heat and divide the pudding into equal portions among flat serving plates. Smooth the tops with a spoon and set aside to cool. Serve at room temperature.

# Sweet Dumplings

## *Awwamaat*

In this Lebanese sweet, small balls of fried dough are soaked in sugar syrup. The Arabic name translates to "one that floats" because the dough bursts to the surface of the oil once fried. It's fun to make as a family cooking project, but you may find they will all be eaten in a matter of minutes.

My husband's family is from a village in Mount Lebanon called Achkout. My father-in-law, Albert, who is 94 years old, often shares memories with me of his childhood. A festival commemorating the town's patron saint, St. Jean the Baptist, was held every summer on the 29th of August. As a child, he would impatiently count down the days, collecting pennies to buy sweets and ice cream in particular, which at that time was a rare treat. The day would come and the scent of frying dough would waft through the churchyard, where vendors showcased all types of sweets and toys. The confectioner would stand in front of a huge frying pan, flipping balls of dough into the hot oil. Albert remembers the *sandook el ferjah*, the cartoon image box, the photographer, the sword swallower, the snake tamer, and the card and thimble players. There would also be tug of war, and competitions in weight lifting and ringing the heavy church bell. The church was open for praying, lighting candles, or making contributions in the offering box, and the whole community came out to wander the fair and take part in the festivities.

1 cup (120 g) all-purpose flour
1 cup (250 g) plain yogurt
¼ teaspoon baking soda
Vegetable oil, for frying
2¾ cups (650 ml) sugar syrup
  (p. 214), or as needed

Beat the flour into the yogurt, add baking soda and then stir until you have a thick batter. Cover the bowl with a kitchen towel and leave to rise for at least 1 hour.

Pour vegetable oil into a large pot or deep-fryer to a depth of 2 in (5 cm). Heat until the oil reaches a temperature of 350°F (180°C) or until small bubbles gather around a small piece of dough dropped into the oil (monitor the oil temperature as you work). Dip a round teaspoon into the oil to stop the dough from sticking, generously fill it with dough, and using another small spoon, slide the dough into the hot oil. Working in small batches, fry balls of dough in this way until golden on all sides (they will float to the surface when done). Using a slotted spoon, transfer to a plate or steel colander lined with paper towels to drain excess oil.

Pour the cool sugar syrup into a large bowl. While still warm, immerse the dumplings in the syrup, stirring gently until they are thoroughly coated. Drain and transfer them to a serving plate. Serve at room temperature.

# Tahini Cookies with Pistachios

*Ka'ak bil Tahini ma' Fustok Halabi*

If you love tahini as much as I do, you will love these rich and nutty cookies. They simply melt in your mouth. I assure you that you will not stop at eating only one. I have cooked Lebanese meals in restaurants around the world and I often made these cookies to end the meal on a sweet note. I would serve Arabic coffee and slide a cookie on the saucer.

7 tablespoons (100 g) unsalted
   butter at room temperature
½ cup (100 g) sugar
⅔ cup (100 g) tahini
½ teaspoon vanilla extract
1 cup (120 g) all-purpose flour
1 teaspoon baking powder
Pinch salt (optional)
10 peeled pistachios, halved
   (or more if needed)

Preheat the oven to 350°F (180°C). Line two baking sheets with parchment paper.

In a mixing bowl or stand mixer, beat the butter and sugar together until light and fluffy. Mix in the tahini and vanilla until smooth.

In another mixing bowl, combine the flour, baking powder, and salt (if using). Gradually mix the dry ingredients into the tahini mixture, mixing between additions until it comes together into a dough.

Transfer the dough to a clean work surface and use your hands to press it into a round.

Form the dough into 20 even balls (this will make 2 in/5 cm cookies, but make smaller ones if you prefer). Arrange on the baking sheets, leaving 2 in (5 cm) of space between them. Gently flatten the balls with the tines of a fork, and push one pistachio half into each one. Bake for 8 to 10 minutes until pale golden and the tops have cracked. Remove from the oven and cool on the baking sheets before transferring to wire racks. They will firm up as they cool.

# Lazy Cake (No-Bake Chocolate Cake)

## *Aleb Helou Chocolata*

This is a rich and delicious cake of crushed cookies bound together with chocolate ganache. This recipe can't be left out of any collection of Beiruti desserts—it is served at nearly every child's birthday party in Lebanon. It's a quick and easy no-bake recipe, and a fun project to share with kids. I warn you, there will be a lot of licked spoons. The main ingredients are Ghandour biscuits, wheat digestive cookies that are a universal part of childhood in Lebanon. They are often also sandwiched with Turkish delight (*lokum*) for a sweet treat after meals.

Growing up, my children's sugar intake was restricted to special occasions or homemade desserts and fruit. I would preach to my friends that too many processed foods are bad for children. We would all gather in a park every day after school with the kids to talk and share stories. Once I was boasting about how I never included processed sweets in my children's lunch bags, and an acquaintance, who is now a very good friend, stood up to tell me that her son Henry came home from school very hungry, despite always having these treats in his lunch. It emerged that my son Albert was eating his goodies every day!

10½ oz (300 g) digestive biscuits or graham crackers

14 oz (400 g) chocolate, cut into chunks (I use dark chocolate with 70% cocoa)

10 tablespoons (150 g) unsalted butter

½ cup (150 g) sweetened condensed milk

Line a loaf pan with wax or parchment paper on all sides and set aside.

Break the biscuits into a mixing bowl and use a pestle to crush them into small bite-size chunks (too big and your cake will be too soft; too small and it will be too firm). Set aside.

In a double boiler (or a heat-safe bowl suspended over a large pot of simmering water), melt the chocolate with the butter and condensed milk over medium heat, stirring frequently. Remove from the heat.

Reserve about ½ cup (120 ml) of the chocolate sauce in a small bowl. Working quickly, stir the crushed biscuits into the remaining chocolate sauce, and gently mix until thoroughly coated. Pour the chocolate mixture into the lined loaf pan, spreading it evenly and pressing it down into the base. Pour the reserved chocolate over the top and spread evenly. Cover with foil or plastic wrap and refrigerate overnight, or for at least 5 hours.

Turn the cake out onto a serving plate and slice into even pieces.

# Semolina Cake

## *Nammoura*

This rich cake is sweet, sticky, moist, crumbly, and yummy! *Nammoura* is popular throughout the Middle East, where it is sometimes known by different names: *harisseh* in Palestine, and *basbousa* in Egypt. It's the perfect sweet to serve with a hot drink for a morning or afternoon gathering. A few bites will suffice—it is rich in texture, and sweet because it is soaked in sugar syrup. Each bite melts in your mouth.

½ teaspoon mastic (Arabic gum,
   see p. 216), optional
1 cup (200 g) sugar
1 cup (150 g) fine semolina
3 cups (500 g) coarse semolina
½ teaspoon salt
1 cup (220 g) butter, softened
4 tablespoons rose water
1 cup (250 g) plain yogurt
1½ teaspoons baking soda
4 tablespoons tahini (or use butter),
   for greasing
About 15 blanched almonds,
   halved, or use pine nuts
2¾ cups (650 ml) sugar syrup
   (p. 214)

In a mortar and pestle, crush the mastic with 1 tablespoon of the sugar until fine and combined.

In a large mixing bowl, combine the fine and coarse semolina, ground mastic, the remaining sugar, and salt. Mix well. Add the butter and, using your fingers, rub it into the semolina mixture until thoroughly mixed. Mix in the rose water, yogurt, and baking soda and mix to make a thick batter. Set aside to rest for 1 hour.

Preheat the oven to 350°F (180°C) and grease the bottom and sides of an 11 by 7 in (28 by 18 cm) brownie pan with the tahini. Spoon in the batter, and spread it evenly. Decorate the top with rows of nuts, traditionally in diagonal rows spaced about 2 in (5 cm) apart.

Bake for about 40 minutes, until golden and firm, or until a tester inserted into the center comes out clean. Remove the cake from the oven and, while still hot, pour in cool sugar syrup to cover the surface of the cake. Set aside for at least 1 hour for the syrup to soak in. Use a sharp knife to cut it into squares or diamond shapes with a nut in the center of each. Serve at room temperature.

# Beirut

*Be she a courtesan, a scholar or a devout,*
*peninsula of noise, colors and gold,*
*pink city of commerce, sailing out like a fleet*
*searching the horizon for the tenderness of a harbor,*
*a thousand times dead and a thousand times revived.*
*Beirut of the thousand palaces, Berytus of the rocks derived,*
*where comers from all over raise their statues,*
*for men to pray, and wars to break out.*
*Its women with their beached eyes that light up at night,*
*and its beggars resembling ancient Pythias.*
*In Beirut every idea has a home.*
*In Beirut every word has a throne.*
*In Beirut we unload thoughts and caravans,*
*buccaneers of souls, priestesses or sultanas.*
*Be she pious, or be she witch,*
*be she both or may she switch,*
*from the sea portal or the Orient fence,*
*be she adored or cursed,*
*be she bloody or blessed,*
*be she innocent or murderous,*
*being Phoenician, Arab or in between,*
*being Levantine with many talents already seen,*
*like those strange flowers so frail on their stems,*
*Beirut is for the Orient the last shrine,*
*where the light of humanity will always shine.*

—Nadia Tueni

**Left:** My father, George Abdeni, was a famous photographer in Beirut during the 1970s and early 1980s. I found this portrait of Nadia Tueni in his photo archive. He remembers the kindness of this woman with nostalgia.

# THANK YOU

Writing a book always involves so many dedicated people. I am grateful to all who collaborated to make this work. Michel Moushabeck, thank you for your encouragement to pursue this book during a most difficult time. You gave me a purpose to move forward, in spite of everything. Helena Zakaria spent hours rummaging through her house to lend me all sorts of objects to make the book look special. Thank you for your trust and generosity. Raymond Yazbeck, your photos make the book even more special, as always. Brady Black, your work inspires me to always use art as a means to change the world. George Abdeni, my father, I feel proud to finally publish one of your photographs in one of my books. Nayla Tueni, your grandmother Nadia Tueni has been the muse for my book through her legacy and work. I hope she would approve. Robert Moughanie and Viviane Tegho, thank you for your time in translating the work of Nadia Tueni into English from French.

Many chefs and small-scale food producers helped to share, cook, and style all the recipes in this book. Tony Rami, I am very grateful for your unconditional, constant support fulfilling all my crazy ideas throughout the years. The Falamanki team was so supportive in helping me with food photography namely: Elie Maalouf, Yamen Mokdad, Siman Siblani, and Jamileh Salameh. It was great fun. Danny El Souri, I will always remember our cooking sessions in Ballouneh. Michel Chibli and Zeinab Kheir at the Grand Meshmosh Hotel, your hospitality and generosity will always be a great part of the making of this work. Habib Hadid and family with Hani Alzein, thank you for making my trip to Tyre so special. Thank you to Ishkhanian Bakery, Al Soussi, Baba Sweets, Harout Tenbelian, Ali Moussa, Rami Salman, and Emma Encarnacion for all your efforts and support.

This book would have been very difficult to produce given the dire situation in Lebanon today if it hadn't been for the support of one of my biggest fans, Nagi Boutros, and Pierre Battikha, CEO of Cortas. Thank you for all the jars that overflowed my kitchen while I tested the recipes.

Maria Massaad, my daughter, thank you for helping me put the puzzle together to make this book, using our common creative vision. It has made all the difference. Leyla Moushabeck you have been so thorough, diligent, and patient in editing this project. I am very grateful to you for pushing me to look at all the minute details to perfect this book. Harrison Williams, your design work reminds me of the garnish that is added to a dish, adding visual impact and flavor. I am very grateful. Wael Jamaledine, you always bring my photos to life and you have been a constant source of support for my projects throughout the years.

Last, but not least, a special thanks to my Abdeni, Massaad, and Slow-Food families, and to all my friends—near and far—for their endless support and encouragement.

# INDEX